Healing Sacred Wounds

While Reclaiming My Power

A Lightworker's Spiritual Insights for Navigating Triggers, Heartbreak, and Higher Consciousness

by V.C. Pitt

ISBN Hardcover #: 979-8-9865366-4-4
ISBN Paperback #: 979-8-9865366-2-0
ISBN Electronic #: 979-8-9865366-3-7
Library of Congress Control Number: 2025914993

Book Cover courtesy of S. Hatcher, photographer
Proofread by Zora Knauf, 2025
PRESStinely, Author Consulting, Book Marketing & Publishing, 2025

Printed in the United States of America.
V.C. Pitt
United States

healingsacredwounds.com

Disclaimer: This book is a memoir. The events and experiences detailed within are true and have been rendered as faithfully as the author remembers them, to the best of her ability. Names and identifying characteristics have been changed and some events have been compressed to protect the privacy of the individuals involved, regardless of whether such changes are identified.

Table of Contents

Acknowledgments vii

Introduction.. ix

Chapter One – Digging Deeper 1
    Divine Feminines 6

Chapter Two – Living Life Post Breast Cancer.................... 13
    My Insurance Fiasco 15
    Charity Run 18
    My Struggle with Weight... 21
    Business Matters.. 22

Chapter Three – Dealing With Trauma, Curses, and
The Dark Feminine 29
    Generational Wounding.. 32
    The Sacred Feminine 35

Chapter Four – Discovering the Supernatural.................... 37
    Intuitive Hit 39
    Supernatural Events.. 40
    High Priestess Modalities... 41
    Tarot 42
    Crystals 43
    Astrology... 44

Chapter Five – Telling the Truth... 47

Chapter Six – Walking into Round One.............................. 53
    Family Christmas 56
    Holiday Gatherings 58

Chapter Seven – Connecting in Sedona 61

Chapter Eight – Falling into Round Two.......................67
  Peace and Healing 69
  A Happy Fall...71

Chapter Nine – Reading From a Spiritual Discerner 75
  Readings...76

Chapter Ten – Matching on a Dating App 83

Chapter Eleven – Meditating and Letting Go....................89
  Brother...91

Chapter Twelve – Having a Perfect First Date....................97

Chapter Thirteen – Achieving Higher Consciousness
During Ayahuasca Journeys...101
  Ayahuasca 103
  Releasing and Forgiving Daddy 106
  Last Daytime Journey..108
  Seeking Spiritual Guidance....................................111
  Finding Healing Crystals.......................................115

Chapter Fourteen – Receiving Divine Protection.............121

Chapter Fifteen – Hoping for Vulnerability.....................129

Chapter Sixteen – Manifesting and Protecting.................135
  Manifestation 137
  Psychic Clarity 137
  Health Crisis 138

Chapter Seventeen – Hearing Three Little Words.............143
  Birthday..145
  Evening Walk...147

Chapter Eighteen – Reuniting.......................................155
  Getting Back Together...156
  Quiet Night at Home...160

Chapter Nineteen – Remembering (Past Life Regression) 163

    Dangerous Weather 164

    Christmas 166

    New Year's Eve with Our Lady's Group 168

    Spiritualists 170

Chapter Twenty – Stepping Away 173

    Mirroring Twin Flame 175

    Winter Bleakness 176

Chapter Twenty-One – Yearning and Burning 179

Chapter Twenty-Two – Fighting the Downward Spiral 187

    The Solar Eclipse 190

    The Turning Point 192

    Elohee Revisited 193

Chapter Twenty-Three – Revisiting the Past 203

Chapter Twenty-Four – Finding Soul Aspects 209

    Tasseography (Tea Leaf Reading) 213

Chapter Twenty-Five – Looking into My Soul 219

Chapter Twenty-Six – Moving Forward 225

    Here We Go Again 227

    Free… at Last 229

    Our Story 231

    Reflection 233

    Closing the Door 234

    Channeling 236

    A New Attitude 238

    Wrapping It Up 239

Epilogue 241

    Mushrooms 241

Appendix 251
    Channeling 251

Bibliography 265

About the Author 267

Acknowledgments

Alex, I'm grateful for our friendship that's developed over the last three years. You've listened to me without judgment and supported me while reading my rough drafts. I'm thankful for you and count you as a true friend.

Sloan, you came into my life unexpectedly. Fate brought us together, and our destiny is for our lives to remain intertwined. You support me and bring joy into my life. I never expected to have a little sister at this stage in my life, but the Divine knew we needed each other. You're my soul aspect and are beautiful inside and out. I'm grateful for your love and friendship. Accept nothing less than you deserve. Let your light shine!

Astrid and Alana, my gorgeous and graceful spiritual sisters, little did I know when I met you how much you would affect my life. You're part of my soul group and are my genuine family. Both of you have changed my life in such a positive way. You have loved, encouraged, and accepted me, even when I struggled to accept myself. I love you both from the bottom of my heart. Sisters, we have much to do spiritually as the power of three. Our love, will, and determination will introduce others to spirituality. I'm blessed that our paths intersected.

Kevin, you're a mirroring Twin Flame whom God brought into my life to teach me lessons. We've repelled and triggered each other. I was stuck in the past, and you helped me move forward, so I'm grateful for that. Even when our road traveled was rocky, you helped me heal. Don't accept toxicity. I hope you do your work and become emotionally healthy. My heart loves you unconditionally.

And to family, friends, and acquaintances not mentioned here who helped me when I was writing this book by reviewing many rough drafts. Your feedback helped me, and I want to extend my deepest gratitude to all of you. Thank you for your support and encouragement.

Introduction

Hey there, beautiful soul.

If you're holding this book, chances are you've been through some stuff. The kind of stuff that breaks you open and leaves you wondering who you are anymore. The kind of stuff that makes people tell you to "just think positive" or "everything happens for a reason"—and you want to throw something at them because they clearly don't get it.

I get it.

Seven years ago, I thought I had life figured out. I was running a successful business, had been married for almost twenty-five years, and was checking all the boxes society tells us we're supposed to check. Then, one day, I slipped getting out of the shower, fell face-first onto tile flooring, and everything changed. That fall didn't just bruise my face—it cracked me wide open spiritually and started an awakening I never saw coming.

What followed was a twin flame affair that ended my marriage, a breast cancer diagnosis, plant medicine journeys that showed me parts of myself I didn't know existed, and a spiritual awakening that's been equal parts devastating and beautiful.

I've made choices I'm not proud of while searching for love in all the wrong places. I've been triggered into what felt like the pits of hell, and I've also discovered I carry the energy of an ancient goddess.

This isn't a book about pretending spiritual awakening is all love and light. This is about what really happens when your soul decides it's time to remember who you are—and it's chaotic.

In these pages, you'll walk with me through breast cancer and insurance nightmares, through Ayahuasca ceremonies that rewrote my understanding of reality, through the discovery that I'm connected to Aphrodite's lineage. You'll see me at my lowest points and witness the moments when divine grace broke through the darkness. You'll learn about twin flames, plant medicine, divine feminine energy, generational trauma, and what it really means to reclaim your power when everything you thought you knew about yourself gets blown apart.

This is the continuation of my story that began in my first book, but it's also a guide for anyone who is tired of spiritual bypassing and ready to do the real work. The work involves facing your shadow, healing generational wounds, and learning to love yourself while navigating supernatural experiences that most people wouldn't believe.

I'm not here to convince you of anything. I'm here to share what happened to me—the ugly parts and the miraculous parts—because someone needs to tell the truth about what spiritual transformation actually looks like. It's not social-media worthy most of the time. It's raw, it's real, and it will change you in ways you never expected.

Whether you're a twin flame, a lightworker, someone dealing with trauma, or just a human trying to figure out why life feels so complicated, this book is for you. You'll discover that you're here on a soul mission that's bigger than anything you imagined.

I've been divinely guided to share this story, even though part of me is terrified of what people will think. But I've learned that when Divine pushes you to do something, resistance becomes impossible. The people who need to hear this message are waiting, and I refuse to let fear keep me from serving my purpose.

So grab your favorite drink, get comfortable, and prepare for a journey that's going to take you places you never expected. This isn't just my story—it's a mirror for your own spiritual transformation, however chaotic and beautiful it might be.

Let's dig deeper together.

With love and light (and a healthy dose of reality),

V.C.

Chapter One

Digging Deeper

When I completed my first book, *My Twin Flame Journey of Separation, Surrender, and Release*, I fulfilled part of my soul's divine mission. This book is a continuation of my spiritual and divine journey, not only as a Twin Flame but also as a lightworker, healer, and Divine Feminine. I've participated in multiple psychedelic journeys, so I'll be delving deeper into plant medicine usage for emotional and physical healing, which has resulted in my spiritual transformation.

Healing Sacred Wounds While Reclaiming My Power was written to help readers look within at what additional healing they need to do to move forward on their own healing journey. This is a story of how unconditional love happened for me after separation from Erick, my Twin Flame. Twin Flames are a past-life spiritual and soul connection who have reincarnated in many past lives together. Twins are two halves of the same soul. We share a soul contract full of lessons, but the longer I'm here, the more I realize it's holy mission work and much bigger than just two people.

I'm on a healing journey, transforming low vibrational energy into high vibrational energy. However, I'm human. Sometimes I can take ten steps forward and two steps back. It's unfortunate, but in the last few months, I continue moving forward with minimal anxiety, minus triggers. That's progress! Even if you aren't a Twin Flame, you may have similar wounding that needs healing.

Many twins are lightworkers and starseeds. Lightworkers commit to carrying more light, love, and higher consciousness to the world. Our positivity is usually felt by others, and we're intuitive and empathic. Starseeds are thought to have come to Earth from another planet or dimension. Their goal is to help humanity and the planet. Starseeds I've met have a distinct appearance, look younger, and have light blue eyes.

Twins are drawn together magnetically. We have spiritual gifts that complement each other. However, our childhood wounding and adult traumas come to the surface, exposed, which can make us trigger and repel each other. My spirituality has advanced partially because of my gifts, and this book shares details of what happened after my first book. The Divine (whom I call simply "Divine") wanted me to share more so others can learn from my experiences. I want to introduce you to the types of spiritual modalities that have enriched my life. Multiple psychic mediums have told me I'd write a second book revealing my journey—and here it is.

As a child, I was sensitive and gentle. My hair was mousy brown, and I had freckles across my nose and cheeks. I have olive green eyes, and my smile is my best feature. Weight became my struggle in fourth grade. After I cut my hair from mid-back length to short in fifth grade, people often mistook me for an overweight boy. Comments made still affect me today. I experienced childhood wounding that included abandonment and rejection, and my self-worth was challenged. Many issues arise as an adult when you don't heal these wounds.

Sometimes wounding leads us to overachieving in our professional life, and that's what happened to me. I excelled while building a successful career and business for over ten years. But then, seven years ago, in 2017, one day, I wasn't feeling well and became dehydrated. I took a shower and became dizzy. It caused me to trip out of the shower, fall, and land on my face on tile flooring. That fall changed me. It started my spiritual awakening, and I became aware of being a Twin Flame. I'd been married almost twenty-five years when I realized I had a soul connection and Twin Flame. Erick was my Certified Business Consultant and my muse. He supported me when I started my medical billing and accounts receivable business and saw me become successful. Our collaboration led to our fiery connection and subsequent all-consuming affair, which resulted in my divorce and my spirit being broken for a period of time. Stressed, I started over—and experienced heartbreak along the way. But I persevered.

Although I can't be sure, I believe stress and emotional triggers led to my breast cancer diagnosis in my early fifties. Luckily, I only had to have a lumpectomy and radiation for that highly aggressive cancer. Now in my mid-fifties, I'm a three-year breast cancer survivor. After cancer and my deepening spirituality, my priorities changed. God is now foremost in my life. I downsized a large part of my medical billing business, and I'm starting my spiritual business this year. My growing spirituality allowed me to recognize I was incomplete without a relationship with God, our Creator. Sometimes I refer to God as Source energy, because God is the loving source of all energy. Some readers may believe that the words I share in this book aren't "of God" because mine is an untraditional story. But those people and characters who are featured in the Bible had hardships and overcame their challenges, too. Like them, I've faced hardships throughout my life, but I refuse to let adversity define me. Hopefully, my story inspires you to learn more about spirituality in a time when Earth is transitioning to New Earth.

People have different interpretations of what the term "New Earth" means. For a long time, I thought the afterlife was a place I'd been taught about at church: Heaven or Hell. As I got deeper into my spiritual awakening and researched lost books of the Bible, I spoke with others like me to put together pieces of a puzzle I'm still researching. I believe there's a positive shift coming to our planet, and collectively we'll remember why we're here. Jesus, the Angels, and Holy and Interdimensional beings are part of that process. After the transition happens, we'll enter a new era here on Earth, where unconditional love is all that is, which is what will result in our redeemed humanity. What I'll share along my journey, of course, is from my perspective alone. I can't put words in my Twin Flame's mouth. I know that twins often have a similar dynamic and attitude overall. For example, usually, one twin is deeply religious (Erick) and the other is highly spiritual (me). A person gravitates toward what they're comfortable with, and their beliefs are their choice. Just as there are different faiths in religion, spirituality has many paths.

Growing up, I attended Granny's Southern Baptist Church, after having been baptized into the Church of Christ. When I was nine, I was at a church camp. Late one night, a classmate got baptized in the lake. Sitting with her and hearing her fears, I got scared that I might not wake up and be saved, so I got baptized, too. Looking back, I was far too young to enter that permanent decision without speaking to my family or understanding what I was agreeing to.

Years later, I didn't know how religious Erick (a cradle Catholic) was until we got involved. As a middle-aged woman, spirituality made more sense to me than religion, and I connected to it fully. As time goes on, I learn more. I'm spiritual, and I have charismatic gifts. Erick is intuitive and empathic, and he's my many-times-past-life connection. He was the catalyst for my spiritual awakening. Even with the heartbreak and triggers I experienced, I'm grateful for our time together. I remembered how to love unconditionally. Through our relationship, I remembered my soul contract and was reminded I needed to do the related healing. I knew I needed to find and step into my Divine Feminine.

There are three concepts that will be discussed within these pages. The soul is who you really are. It's the part of you that feels like "you." Your soul holds your deepest truths, your purpose, and all the wisdom from your life experiences. Spirit is our connection to something bigger than self. It's that feeling you get when you're in nature, or when you feel deeply loved, or when everything just feels magical and connected. Spirit is the energy that flows through you and connects you to everything else. Our higher self is your wisest inner voice. It's the part of you that always knows what's right, even when your worried mind is spinning. It's like having your own personal guide who sees the bigger picture, guides you, and loves you unconditionally. When I talk about these concepts in my journey, I mean the different ways I came to understand myself, not just as this person dealing with daily life but as an eternal being having a human experience, connected to everything, with access to wisdom I didn't even know I had.

Divine Feminines

"Divine Feminines" are the architects and seem to be farther along spiritually than "Divine Masculines," who are the builders. Feminines get visions and downloads, and their intuition guides them to be in service to God and the Collective. Masculines support the Feminines in their endeavors and help carry out God's plan. Right now I'm co-creating with others in the collective of what I hope will be the result when New Earth is here. When the Masculine and Feminine are in separation and one of the two pulls away, the other shoulders the responsibility of both parts by balancing the masculine and feminine energy within themselves. It's much easier to do this when you have love for yourself.

Also, I send unconditional love out while grounding to help heal our planet and usher in higher timelines. I create using my intuitive gifts (clairsentience, clairaudience, clairvoyance, and claircognizance) to accomplish the divine plan (God's will). Those gifts are from both grandparents through my maternal lineage.

When I get an intuitive hit, I get chills on the tops of my upper thighs, which lets me know my hit's correct. Part of my soul contract is teaching others about spirituality and unconditional love, so I try to share my focus, my mission. Once Feminines like me become clear on what they want to manifest and create, the Masculines are to support us in our endeavors.

Plato, a Greek philosopher, discussed the mythology of Twin Flames in his dialogue "The Symposium." (An excerpt is available to read online.) In Greek mythology, twins were androgynous beings with a head with two faces, looking opposite ways, set on a round neck. They had four ears, four arms, and four legs. Zeus, king of the Olympian gods, feared the twins' power, and he ordered them to split into separate parts, condemning the beings to spend their lives searching for their other halves.

In modern times, spiritual communities that explore the theory of twins often discuss ancient myths featuring stories of twins. For example, the Egyptian goddess Isis and her twin brother and husband, Osiris, are considered Twin Flames. They had a passionate relationship, resulting in a tragic love story. Their brother, Set, jealous of Osiris, wanted Osiris' throne. Set killed and dismembered Osiris. Devastated, in intense grief, Isis wandered Egypt and beyond, searching for his remains so she could reassemble them.

Isis and Osiris' story echoes Twin Flames' yearning and searching for their twin soul. If they find them, they can experience love, friendship, and soul growth. While some twins can feel incomplete if they're apart, not all twins have romantic connections. It depends on your soul contract this lifetime with one another. A soul contract is a relationship between souls that's agreed upon before reincarnating to Earth. Our soul contract contains the lessons we will work on during our current life, and it allows us to clear karma from our previous life. The more often a soul has reincarnated, the more complicated the web of design is. People you encounter who feel familiar are souls who have a soul contract with you—especially if they trigger you. And, of course, we all have free will and choice, which complicates matters!

Some souls are new, while others have been here for different time periods. I believe souls are created from energy. Twin souls were created at the same moment, with the same particles of energy, and are some of the oldest souls on Earth. In the non-physical plane, there's a library archive of memories, events, and knowledge called the Akashic Records (the Akasha). According to my Akashic Records, my soul has experienced many lifetimes, including lives in ancient Egypt, China, and Persia.

In our soul contracts, before we incarnate, we choose our family and the lessons we want to learn. Often, twins experience similar wounding in childhood, which is highlighted when, as adults, when we encounter each other. Repressed feelings come to the surface and expose those wounds like a raw nerve. During our healing, we often repel our twin as we learn our lessons and express ourselves. Our healing is about working through the wounding. We harmonize all parts of our soul so we're in alignment and complete (whether or not we're together).

Physical union isn't always part of a twin soul's soul contract. Accepting this helped me focus on what I'm to do while here on Earth. I accepted I may never be healed fully, but I'm hopeful and continue working toward that goal. For me, constant intense triggers pull me to my shadow side, and when this happens, desperation, isolation, and emotional destruction spiral me into grief. My world implodes. It's as if I don't matter. The intensity of separating from my Twin Flame is overwhelming. I try to not get sucked into the darkness, but sometimes I can't avoid a trigger. I've been caught in repetitive loops. However, in recent months, I've broken this cyclic pattern.

In the past, I've had irrational thoughts that have made me isolate myself. When this blackness overtakes me, no one in my sphere understands my internal pain. I've hidden in drugs and alcohol, indulged in casual sexual relationships, and have even left town to avoid and escape the pain. But all of it is only a temporary fix.

While in this destructive energy, I grip the handle on a spinning merry-go-round, trying to avoid being thrown off. My mind swirls into instant, overwhelming anxiety and impending doom. It's as though the spotlight is on me, and I'm unprepared to deliver a speech to thousands of people. My inner child wants to be loved, held, and protected. It's an inevitable "Tower Moment," and it's devastating. (In Tarot, when the Tower card is revealed during a reading, it's a chaotic or painful crisis moment where someone is experiencing a sudden or unexpected change. After the moment of destruction, the Tower card foreshadows breakthrough and the opportunity for a fresh start after a difficult time.)

My Twin-Flame triggers have lessened over the past five years. Still, I experience mini-triggers—watered-down, less painful versions of what I've experienced in the past. Some people might call these experiences depression, anxiety, or panic attacks. They're none of these things. My friends know that as a Virgo, I retreat into what I refer to as Hermit mode. In the Tarot, the Hermit card represents Virgos, inner guidance, soul searching, wisdom, spiritual enlightenment, and solitude. When I'm in Hermit mode, I don't answer the door, answer phone calls, or reply to texts. I give those closest to me a heads up (so no one worries) and retreat into my inner world for safety and protection. No one takes it to heart—they know this is how I am.

Sometimes the anguish and despair I experienced in these dark moments were more than I could bear, but I forced myself to move forward. My triggers come in waves, which pulled me into the pits of hell. Six years after Erick left, my sleep cycles remain inconsistent. For years, I've slept only five or six hours at night (if I'm lucky). I think stress, triggers, and lack of sleep were some of the factors that led to my developing breast cancer. (I'll talk about that later.)

On many nights, I sat in my brown leather chair until midnight because I didn't want to be alone in my bed. Images and memories of Erick replayed in my mind. Sometimes, I felt my energy with Erick and remembered him next to me. Erick discovered my deeply sensual side. He feels like home. His leaving me remained a PTSD-event for me. I missed our intimacy, connection, and sensuality, and skin-on-skin contact.

I realized that learning to be alone was my newest lesson. Loneliness is something I've never done well. There's a difference between being alone and being lonely. We all need to be alone from time to time. In the winter months, with their short days, my loneliness is worse than at any other time. My desire for love and romance in my life is strong, and that's where most of my loneliness lies. I'm not sure if I'm meant to be with someone long term for my remaining days, but I'm holding out for the right man to come into my life.

Along my path, there have been spiky peaks and dark abysses. I made the mistake of seeking love through sex. I experimented and engaged in casual sexual practices that some people might consider dangerous. (But I never compromised my safety. I always let those closest to me know where I was.) However, I was out of control and wanted to change… to return to my truest essence. Also, I was tired of my breasts being the first thing people noticed about me when I walked into a room. I scheduled surgery and wanted to modify both my physical appearance and behaviors.

I had a "mommy makeover" (a cosmetic breast reduction and lift, abdominoplasty, and liposuction). I was ready to make changes. I no longer discounted myself. My moral compass returned front and center. I no longer pursue casual relationships. Remembering my worth and growing spiritually has allowed me to work on healing my self-worth.

For me to be attracted to a man (beyond his looks), there has to be a deep spiritual connection. Most men won't accept my beliefs or handle how strong a Divine Feminine I am. Many men aren't as spiritual as I am, and I refuse to accept a status-quo relationship. I'm loving and easy-going, yet complex. Why can't I have the happiness so many people experience? Why do I seek complicated men and situations? It's because Divine has other plans for me—to heal myself and to work on my spirituality and past-life karma.

Three winters ago, I told myself I wouldn't spend another winter alone in my bed. I see countless women who possess the self-love to find happiness in solitude, and I go to many places unaccompanied, relishing the freedom coveted by others. I've spent a large amount of time alone. It's part of my self-worth lesson and how I'm wired, although I know I must love myself as much as I love others. That's a huge part of why we're here: to love ourselves, but I didn't for a long time. I still ask myself,

"Why do I crave love so much?" Everyone loves differently. For me, love is all-encompassing, like it was between Erick and me.

At the end of my first book, I thought I'd pulled myself free from my connection with Erick. The dynamic between twins is a push/pull force, and I couldn't break free long term from our magnetic attraction. It always pulled me back in. Unless you're a Twin Flame, it's difficult to comprehend what many onlookers would consider an obsession. It's like an addiction, but there's no fix to provide relief. As I continue to release my attachment to the outcome in our journey, I stand by my faith in the Divine. I know that if Erick isn't returning, the Divine will bring someone in who's a close vibrational match to me. I've tried to be patient, and while that isn't always my virtue, in the past year, I've come a long way.

As I think back to the time after my Twin Flame affair with Erick ended, many feelings arise. They come and go. After our affair, I got together with and broke up with other men. I was hurt, and those relationships were distractions—I was missing Erick and our spiritual connection. As hard as it is for me to admit, Erick disposed of me, which caused sadness in my soul and activated my deepest wound: rejection. If you're in or recovering from a Twin Flame relationship, I hope you're no longer stuck, as I was. In time, I learned to move forward and smile. You can, too!

After I published my first book, synchronicities involving Erick started happening and have continued for over eight years. For me, synchronicity includes seeing numbers or symbols (license plates and billboards), clairaudiently hearing songs (many I've never heard of from the 1970s), having dreams with conversations, and experiencing situations that remind me of Erick and our connection. For example, when I was promoting my first book, I drove to metaphysical bookstores. When I arrived at the first local store I visited, I saw Erick's birthday written numerically on a license plate. I saw it again later in a vehicle parked at the last bookstore I visited. In numerology, both our life path numbers are 7 and 9, so 79 remains prominent for me, and I see that number often.

For four years, the number 34 has been my constant companion, but I'm still unsure of what it represents. When I see 3479 or 7934, I'm reminded of my soul contract with Erick, and I try to comprehend the message the numbers are sending me. These repeating sequences give you awareness and direction on your journey. Seeing them is a nod acknowledging you're on the right path. I'm doing my inner healing work, but my intuition tells me (and psychic readers and mediums say) that Erick isn't doing his.

Chapter Two

Living Life Post Breast Cancer

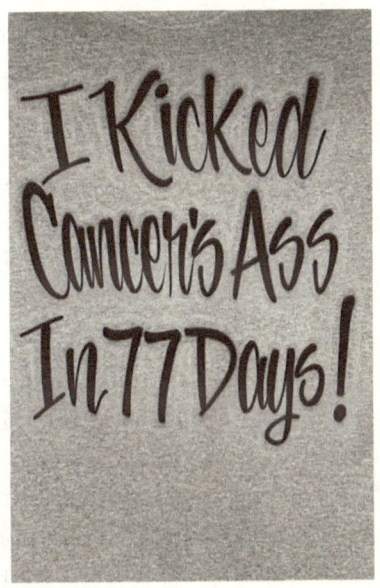

In *My Twin Flame Journey*, I shared my struggles with numbing out using alcohol. It's been two years since I've had a drink. One day, after ordering two doubles at a bar (which cost me forty dollars), I was sick for a day. I told myself, "There's no need to drink anymore. It doesn't make me happy. It's an expense with a hangover." Tapping into my maturity and concentrating on healing broke my cycle of drinking to escape my problems. Sometimes, when I reflect on my past cycles, it's like reviewing someone else's actions.

Before my cancer treatment, I'd stopped smoking pot. When I had my first radiation treatment, I had severe anxiety and panic attacks. A friend sent me a care package that included a THC vape pen, but I didn't plan on using it. By the second day of treatment, I was having severe panic attacks with adrenaline spikes. I knew I couldn't endure all the treatment without something to calm me, so I got high in my car or outside in the parking lot. I found using THC calmed me down and helped me sleep. It was a crutch I needed during that scary period—and it's a viable option when someone doesn't need regular anxiety or depression medication.

When I was in high school, I was judgmental about anyone who smoked pot. The first time I smoked THC was the night before my twenty-second birthday. Then, before I got pregnant, I stopped and didn't pick it up again for over twenty years. I now use marijuana medicinally. It's a tool to help us, but I've decreased my use of it this year.

As those who have read my first book know, I enjoy working with the psychedelic plant medicine Ayahuasca and have experienced many other-worldly healing journeys. In an Ayahuasca retreat, one lies on a mat in an outdoor arena or a comfortable inside space, and the shaman or practitioner brings the medicine to each participant, who drinks the potion and remains on their mat for the duration of the experience. (I'll refer to these experiences as "at Ayahuasca.")

Ayahuasca is a sacred ceremony. The sacrament you drink is a plant-based tea, also known as DMT, which produces a psychedelic response. It activates parts of the brain associated with memory, emotion, intention, and visual perception. Over a two-year period, I took part in nine day and night ceremonies at Soul Quest in Orlando, Florida (which has since closed). Most of those ceremonies were after my breast cancer.

During my Ayahuasca travels, when I relax, I'm given "light code" images through my third eye. The codes aren't actual Egyptian hieroglyphics or Inca, Aztec, or Mayan symbols, but these are the only things I can compare the codes to. I believe these images are embedded in me so I can recall my past—all of which will assist me in helping others in the future. Since my ninth Ayahuasca journey, the light codes, which represent ancient wisdom, have continued to appear when I vape THC.

As I journeyed with Aya, my vibrational level elevated to the Fifth Dimension. Our 3D is the physical world, materialism (what's real), while 5D is a higher vibration, interconnectedness (oneness) where one feels unconditional love and peace. It's a wonderful, encompassing feeling.

As I mentioned, since my radiation treatments, I've used a vape pen, which I know isn't the healthiest habit. Other than vaping marijuana, I have no other vices—well, except for using profanity and eating sugar! I've picked THC up again, but I stop when planning to take part in an Ayahuasca ceremony, as participants must abstain from all intoxicants three weeks before attending a ritual.

My Insurance Fiasco

I'm grateful to be given the gift of longer life post-breast cancer. After being diagnosed, I was in shock. I looked at what my benefits and costs might be and had a "holy crap" moment. I discovered that the insurance coverage I'd taken out a year earlier was a discount plan instead of a traditional healthcare insurance plan. That meant that services were "covered," but insurance only paid a small portion of the bills, so I had to pay the patient responsibility part. My policy only paid $2,000 toward my surgery and four office visits. I reached out to my business consultant, Mark, for advice. There were so many financial uncertainties. He recommended I sign up for Healthcare Exchange insurance. Overwhelmed by receiving a cancer diagnosis and making healthcare decisions, when I did contact them, I was a week overdue for eligibility.

It went from bad to worse. I'd chosen the worst healthcare plan for my situation and had to live with it. My income is over 400 percent above the poverty level, so I received no financial help. I reached out to several breast cancer fundraising organizations and at every turn was told I wasn't eligible. On top of not knowing if I'd live or die, I had to contend with financial devastation. I was in a money-loss shock. I've never experienced that level of hopelessness. After the damage was done—after surgery, the physician, the hospital, the radiation, the diagnostic testing, the lab work, the pathology, the radiology, and the other costs—I owed $134,500.00. I was trying to climb Mount Everest to pay bills. I'd enjoyed financial abundance for several years, but that was over.

I believe this financial challenge was karma from my affair, divorce, and the actions I'd taken during that period of my life. But luckily, I had a bit of money I'd saved from Mama's estate funds, savings from my work earnings, and personal money I'd set aside, so I had a bit of cushion.

When I received each statement for medical services, I reconciled it against any payments I'd made and compared it to the explanation of benefits of services. There can be bill discrepancies, so if you're ever in this situation, I recommend comparing these three pieces of information. I found many mistakes in the statements, so I reached out to whomever had sent the bill and had the error corrected. Also, I asked each provider, "If I pay each balance all at once, would you give a prompt payment discount?" Several organizations did. My surgeon ordered gene testing to see what cancers I was at risk for. After the claim was processed, I had a $5,000 balance due. But when I called to make payment arrangements, I discovered my gene testing balance had been written-off by the lab. I was blessed.

Around this time, the doctor with the large office I work with lost a major insurance contract and feared the insurance company would want to recoup monies paid to the office, which, in turn, would've affected my livelihood. I wrote myself a smaller paycheck from my business checking account, and that allowed me to save additional money in my business account, in case money had to be returned to the insurance company. When I received my radiation bill, I owed $76,000 (part of the $134,500). I reached out, and the company offered me a 30 percent discount if I'd pay it in full, which I did. It was a hard pill to swallow, ending up in this situation. But despite having been unaware of the intricacies of my medical plan, I'm knowledgeable about how the administrative side of healthcare works. Looking back, paying myself less was a blessing in disguise. My intuition let me know this change was divinely orchestrated so I could pay my radiation bill.

Because I'm alone, and had no additional estate funds coming, I didn't know how I'd recover from this grand mess or how long my new anxiety about finances would continue. I stopped going to the store as often. First, I cut out luxuries. Then, it got to the point where I couldn't even buy necessities. I had little food in my kitchen cabinets. I skipped meals so I didn't spend money. I ignored my stomach when it growled. As a diabetic, my blood sugar spiked. I'd worked hard and was afraid of losing it all. Between all of this, and having to clear Mama's estate, I became unattached to possessions.

I depended on my credit card more. Selling personal items to pay credit card bills helped me keep my head above water. Nobody knew the full truth of how hard it was for me financially, and I wouldn't ask for help. It wasn't pride as much as I didn't want anyone feeling sorry for me or to feel burdened. I no longer bought clothing or personal items unless they were from a thrift store. Now, I'm far detached from the "American Dream"—and from pride or ego.

Friends suggested I apply for Medicaid benefits and help through the Breast and Cervical Cancer Prevention and Treatment Act. Many recommended reaching out to different organizations that assist, and I did. There were no monies available to me, because you have to be near poverty level to receive help. Some said I should create a GoFundMe account. There was no way I was asking anyone to give me money. I'm already beyond blessed.

I tried to get the hospital to discount my surgery bill so I could put this all behind me. However, they didn't work with me. They said that if I wouldn't agree to making payment arrangements of $700 per month, they would send me to collections. At the time of this writing, I'm still waiting for them to send me to collections.

Now, three years later, the only balance owed is $26,000.00 for my hospital bill. I'm still adjusting my finances to live simply. It's been difficult. I budget. Sometimes there are hiccups, but so far, I can manage. My anxiety over my bills has lessened. But after cancer, things are different. My stamina isn't what it once was. Whereas once I was a workhorse, I can no longer work forty hours a week. I can't exert myself mentally, as I once could. There are days I must take a nap (and I don't feel guilty).

After having a lumpectomy and radiation treatments, I knew I'd live more fully—God gave me extra time. In the first few weeks after radiation, I looked pale and was tired, but after a couple of months, all that subsided.

Charity Run

As I revealed in the epilogue in my first book, I planned to take part in a charity run, which benefits the fight against breast cancer. It looked like fun—even though I hate being dirty and sweaty. I bought a ticket. The day of the run was four months after my radiation ended. I had doubts. "Can I do this when my body has been through so much in a few months?"

I decided, *I'm going to try.*

In the days leading up to the run, I'd increased my walking distance so I could get stronger. Still, I felt weak— radiation takes a toll on your body. One month after my last radiation treatment, I took part in an Ayahuasca ceremony. *If I do that,* I thought, *I can try each obstacle on the charity run.* It was important to me to give others diagnosed with cancer hope. Two cousins, wanting to support me, signed up, too.

Right before the run, I purchased a costume. Many women wear pink breast cancer costumes, and the clothing allows groups to show their support of those in active treatment or who are survivors. As a cancer survivor, I wanted to look strong for the run. I ordered a grey airbrushed tee shirt, which said, "I kicked cancer's ass in 77 days." Besides the tee shirt, I wore a pink tutu, black shorts, sneakers, and a breast cancer buff.

It was early summer, and the day for the run arrived. It was sunny and hot. There was sisterhood with all the other "pink ladies." My cousins and I each applied our temporary black participation tattoos to one thigh. Prior to the start, there was comedic entertainment. The man who was speaking saw my shirt and, over the intercom, he asked, "Are you a survivor?"

I replied, "Yes."

The women around me smiled.

The organizers split the participants into different waves by start time. There were at least one hundred women in my wave, which included my cousins and me. We started the run with others and knew which ladies were a part of a group because they wore the same costumes. It was a sea of pink sisters that day; however, it was more of a walk for me. I completed the first obstacle, a small balance beam, without any problems. The second obstacle was a swing across a muddy hole. I didn't calculate the correct part of the rope to grab onto to swing across, and landed in the mudhole. *So graceful.* We climbed a tall hill. Winded, I had to stop to catch my breath several times. There were mud hills to climb, a mud pond to slide into, and weights to carry. I was a muddy mess! It was so much fun.

There was another mud hole covered by a cargo net. As I crawled under the net, I was on my back, submerged. I tried to keep my mouth above the water. I got muddy water in my ears—yuck. I made it through, but couldn't get a footing to pull myself out of the hole. My cousins pulled me out. I don't think I could've gotten out of there by myself!

For some of the other obstacles, I needed help. The heat exhausted me. By the time I'd exerted myself, my energy was low, and I was shaky. Toward the end, there was a tall cargo net you had to climb up, go over, and navigate your way back down to the ground. It was twelve feet off the ground, with only a thin mat below. I froze because I'm afraid of heights. But my cousins encouraged me. "You've got this," they said. Those words helped me through my fear to complete the obstacle.

When I finished the entire course, I ran across the finish line. The photos taken show me laughing. The smile on my face was priceless. All the participants were filthy but accomplished warriors. After having crawled through the mud and a rocky area, my knees were numb, and the rocks and mud had rubbed the top skin layer off my knees. We sprayed ourselves off, changed our clothes, dragged our poor, tired bodies home.

That day is one I won't forget. I no longer have to shave my knees—the hair there never grew back. Ibuprofen helped my aching muscles some, but for three days, my whole body hurt from the sheer physical exertion. To get the mud out of my hair, I washed it three times. If you'd told me in my younger years I'd do this, I would have laughed at you and said, "No way." I was out of my comfort zone, but I had an amazing time.

Since that time, I've done two more charity runs and have one planned for this year. I'm getting older, but will continue taking part as long as I can.

I'm proud of myself.

My Struggle with Weight

After there was no evidence of cancer remaining, doctors recommended I take Tamoxifen, an estrogen-blocking medication, daily for five years to reduce my risk of recurrence. I started taking it three months after the radiation ended. My tumor gene testing showed the distant recurrence risk at three percent at nine years. It means that if I take the medicine for five years, my chance of breast cancer coming back is only three percent. At first, after picking up the Tamoxifen prescription, I couldn't muster the courage to take it. It sat on my counter a few days before I took the first pill. The side effects of weight gain, brain fog, and joint pain worried me. But I took it, and so far, it's been thirty-six months and I've had no ill effects.

I've worked on creating a healthier lifestyle, embracing life, and moving forward. I'm not taking a single day for granted. If the cancer returns, I won't have regrets. I'm living life. Life isn't living me. What I learned is that when you change your mindset, anything is possible.

I'm just under 5'5," and I've struggled with weight my entire life. Having had body dysmorphia at 125 pounds in my teens, I followed fads, including liquid diets, diet pills, skipping meals, and starving myself. I've had bulimia. I've yo-yoed my weight for thirty-five years, and at my largest, I was 206 pounds. Sugar is my addiction, and nothing made me happier than having extra helpings of dessert. I used to sneak cookies or an extra slice of cake or pie when no one was looking.

Sugar causes inflammation in our bodies. I had pitted edema on my ankles. I struggled with walking my dog, Crystal, and being out of breath. My rings no longer fit my swollen fingers. Shopping and trying to find clothing to fit my apple shape was nearly impossible. I no longer looked like me and avoided the mirror because my body was wide and my face was fat. My cholesterol was high, and my diabetes made me shake because of changes in my blood sugar levels.

I tried different exercises, but nothing worked until I maintained a consistent program of walking. I never thought I'd return to a healthy weight, but in the past eight years, I've lost over sixty pounds. It took being miserable for me to have a permanent lifestyle change. I'm at ease with my new shape. If I didn't have job flexibility with my business, I wouldn't be able to walk as often, so I'm grateful for this.

Business Matters

Having a business required hard work and dedication. I learned how to work hard at school—I was an average student who struggled in school but always wanted to be on the honor roll. Sometimes I made it. Other times I didn't. Mama never thought I'd be a successful business owner because I didn't graduate from college and I didn't excel at anything.

Some might say I attended the School of Hard Knocks when I began working for minimum wage at age seventeen as a nursing assistant. I went to community college for a semester but knew I wasn't cut out for a degree program. At eighteen, I attended a vocational school, excelled, and received a hospital unit clerk certification. After that, I worked at more than one job concurrently, including being a medical records clerk during the week and at a printing company on the weekends. It was tiring working seven days a week, but I discovered my passion for the administrative side of healthcare, particularly medical billing. I got promoted to billing medical claims. Having a natural talent for billing, I found problems and provided solutions. I became efficient at providing the management's desired results. Not everyone can multitask, but I made it look easy. Later, I was an office manager and my superiors would often place me in the spotlight, which made me uncomfortable. They wanted others to provide results using my methods, and the others resented me for it.

A few years after I started my family, I stepped away from the medical field and worked part-time as a legal secretary for a few years. While working for the attorney, I became aware of a medical coding class and decided to become a Certified Professional Coder (CPC). Six months after starting the class, I received my CPC credential. Just as doctors and nurses choose their specialty path, medical coders do the same. I'm not the best coder, but I'm an excellent biller. Combining the two isn't something everyone can do. After a stint of working as a urology coder and later as a Medicare fraud investigator, I wanted to get ahead financially.

My desire to help physicians earn what they were entitled to financially was deep. I transitioned and worked as a receptionist at the front desk in a medical office. After I received another job offer, I left and then worked in the business office for another medical practice. As a Virgo, I have perfectionistic tendencies. When I realized my talent, I used my skill set to advance myself and could bill medical claims 99 percent error-free. My biggest work skill is looking at a doctor's claim charges, reviewing them for any errors, and making corrections. Errors stand out to me, and I'm precise.

After I submit claims, the physicians receive their payments quickly, which keeps the doctors happy. None of the doctors I have worked for are owned by another company. They are able to remain financially independent. I capitalized on my talent and worked for multiple offices. Doctors discussed how I turned their accounts receivable (AR) around quickly. They contacted me, wanting me to help them.

One pulmonology office had $800,000 in AR outstanding. Within three months of working in my first independent contractor job ten hours a week, I'd reduced the AR to $8,000. I was a cash cow for practices. I began to eat, drink, and breathe my job, and generated millions of dollars from billing submissions and streamlined payments. I treated their business as if I had ownership of it. That brought me great satisfaction. It was during this time that I found self-worth through my job; unfortunately, that's just a 3D thing.

I hoped to start my business and benefit from being more than an employee or independent contractor. I was working with Erick, and he completed the LLC paperwork to help me start my own business. I put my business ahead of my family for a long time. After growing my business for five years, it flourished beyond what I'd ever considered possible. My workload and the number of offices I worked in increased by word of mouth without advertising. Mama saw me rise through career challenges, lived to see my success, and was proud of me.

Since I'm intuitive, I used my clairsentience gift (the gut feeling) to my advantage and grew my business. Doctors learned to listen to me when I said, "My gut says… " I've had that spiritual gift since I was a teenager.

A pain management doctor asked me to be his billing manager. He said he was one month from having to sell the business because his profit margin was low. I felt apprehensive but increased his monthly earnings by 1,900 percent in less than two years. I added contractors to my business and eventually transitioned us from working in the pain management office to my home office.

At the height of my career, I was interviewed and a case study was completed on me by the large clearinghouse that I submit claims to. They were impressed with my ability to submit claims 99 percent error free each month for four offices. Our electronic medical record company had a national convention around that time, and the clearinghouse was a sponsor. The clearinghouse asked me to be on their panel discussion at the convention. I surprised myself by speaking easily and was totally in my element.

All that changed when I had my physical fall, which led to my fiery affair with Erick, who served as the catalyst for my spiritual awakening. When something profound happens, it changes you. It's something unstoppable, similar to a tornadic force. It's hard to admit, but after Erick and I connected, he's all I could think of. When a Twin Flame awakens you, obsessive thoughts of the twin engulf you. It's a push/pull dynamic you can't escape—it's unlike anything I've ever experienced. It's part of the journey that others like me face.

After Erick's wife discovered our affair, the ladies who worked in my business with me saw me spiral out of control, being nearly destroyed by waves of triggers. They sympathized and worried—I was broken, my heart shattered. My work suffered, but I continued doing my best, given the circumstances.

When insurance companies changed their reimbursements on procedures performed in the large pain management office, my once-profitable business's revenue decreased. I'm paid a percentage of collections in each office, so if the doctor makes money, so do I. If he makes less money, so do I. However, one doctor listened to his horrible practice manager and a corrupt doctor, and as a result, he lost his insurance contract with a major insurance payer. Later, he apologized to me because he hadn't listened to my recommendations. After spending $300,000 on attorney fees, he regained the contract. By this time, the financial damage was done. I'd never be highly profitable in the pain management office again.

Cancer has changed me. I no longer had it in me to fight and be a workhorse, as I once had. A few years earlier, Erick had told me that if anything goes wrong in the pain management office, financially or otherwise, to pull out and cut my losses. Around this time, insurance companies decreased the number of spinal injection levels that were paid. That office was my business' bread and butter. Because I paid my independent contractors well, and I wouldn't freeze pay increases because I feel financial merit is important and necessary for morale and production, raises would continue. I'd boxed myself into a corner with little opportunity to continue making a decent profit and survive. I spoke with my business consultant, Mark, over my concerns, and he agreed I needed to transition that part of my business. With some rearrangement of resources, within three weeks, the ladies who had been contractors in my business were transitioned to full-time employees for the pain management doctor. Fortunately, I still work independently with three doctors' offices from my home office, which pays my bills.

Part of the loss of the pain management office was my fault. I'd been less passionate about the job, but I also felt defeated after cancer. Looking back, I know that divine intervention brought about the change, because my spiritual path was unfolding. Because of that, I'm not angry. It is what it is. The pressure has decreased. I work at home twenty-five to thirty hours a week.

Although no longer making as much money, I've lived more and traveled some, and I've accepted my situation. Changes in my schedule allow me to think, walk, and pray more, focus on my spirituality, and take naps as I need to. Since the change, my townhouse is too big for me. I've looked for a smaller home closer to Sadie, my beloved cousin, who has become my second mother. Ted, Sadie's son, and his family live next door to Sadie, and I want to be near them.

My biggest lesson is that I accepted what is. I'm not bitter. I've embraced a humble lifestyle and appreciate my blessings. Accomplishment is wonderful, but situations can change. Nothing prepares you for the rug being pulled from under you. For me, that was cancer followed by the loss of the biggest part of a business I was once passionate about—a business I'd created, loved, and built. This loss was ego death. But now I know it's much easier to go with the flow than fight to prevent what will be. Work no longer defines me, and there's hardly any stress, so I consider myself blessed.

Since my financial hemorrhage, unexpected accidents and sickness still happen sometimes. I evaluate whether I need medical care beyond the physicians I work with. For example, I fell and hit the back of my head on several steps at home and went to the emergency room. Happily, there were no adverse effects, other than bruising and soreness. Recently, I had an allergic reaction with hives and went to an urgent care center. The doctor was unsure of what had caused it but asked what I'd eaten. My lunch had included a hamburger, but I eat those at least twice a month, so that seemed unlikely to cause my reaction. After Benadryl, my hives went away. Whenever I go to a facility, I dread knowing the medical bill is coming. However, I take care of my health and pay those bills when I receive them. Just know that your health and financial situation can change instantly, but you can get through it by trusting in our Creator.

Chapter Three

Dealing With Trauma, Curses, and The Dark Feminine

Something I didn't address fully in my earlier book—it's part of the Twin Flame drama I must heal—was the trauma Daddy caused. As a child, I witnessed how vicious he could be toward Mama, especially concerning her weight. I was unaware of some of his cruelty toward her until four years after her death.

Mama was gentle, sweet, kind, and plus sized with a pretty face. Mama's first cousin, Sadie, told me that when Mama was pregnant with my older brother Brian, Daddy pushed her out of their full-sized bed because of her growing belly. Daddy's anger was unpredictable, especially when he was drunk. Some nights he'd come home after I was in bed. He'd check on me, and to avoid him, I'd pretend to be asleep. In my earliest memories, I saw him torment Mama and heard her cries. I was a sensitive child, and experiencing all that contributed to my adult lack of self-worth and body dysmorphia.

At age four, Mama asked me to pack some clothes so we could stay with Grandmother Frances, Daddy's mother, for a few days. It was an adventure for me. The reality I didn't understand was Daddy had beaten Mama, leaving bruises all over her body. She could hardly stand. She needed a break from his abuse.

One morning when I was nine, Daddy asked Mama to prepare hoe cakes for dinner. Mama was working, and she forgot and made cornbread instead. Luckily, Brian and I had already eaten. Daddy leaned into the kitchen table and flung the plates of food off the table onto the floor.

As an adult in my forties, I pulled away from Daddy and Brian. A few years later, when Mama passed away, she excluded Brian and a stepsister from her will. Two years after her death, I found out from Sadie that right before her death, while still in the hospital, Mama had called Brian to tell him she'd updated her will to exclude him. After Mama's death, Daddy told Brian that if it were him, he would sue me personally over it. That was a hard pill to swallow, and I was angry at Daddy while he was still alive. I could almost hear him spew his anger through those words. But Mama's will showed clearly that Brian and my stepsister had, in fact, received their portion of inheritance during Mama's lifetime. When Daddy died eight months after Mama, my half-brother said Brian and I had both been eliminated from Daddy's will. After my stepmother passes away, my half-brother and stepbrother will inherit their estate proceeds and land. It never bothered me, because even though I knew Daddy's last days were near, I had no desire to reconcile with him. I refused to be a pawn in Daddy or Brian's lives and walked away from Daddy's and Brian's toxic behaviors with no regret.

My family's wounding shaped me. Although Daddy caused most of my self-worth wounding, Mama inflicted my abandonment wound when she left us and moved out of the state—without telling me (more on this later). Brian added to my trauma by abusing me emotionally, mentally, and sometimes physically. As a younger sister, I'd looked up to Brian. He's been out of my life for ten years because of his addictions, lies, and behaviors. When I was young, I wanted his love, but he'd talk down to me, do things in front of his friends to make me feel stupid, and sometimes, he'd torment me for the fun of it. For example, once, when I was five, Brian wanted to play football in the house. He tackled me on purpose, knocking the breath out of me. When I was nine, I lay on our green vinyl couch when he pointed his BB gun at me. I smiled and said, "You won't do it." He shot me in the stomach. Although it didn't pierce my skin, I remember the stinging. I won't trust him again or have him in my life. He's always manipulated me.

I was afraid of both Brian and Daddy. When I was twenty, while I was visiting Granny's home, Brian arrived stoned. Granny and I met him outside. He was angry and volatile. Scared he was going to hit Granny, I stepped in front of her. He roughly shoved me to the ground. Thirty-five years later, I can still remember the wild look in his eyes. I was shaken and tried not to cry. He stormed off and drove away. It took me fifty years to stand up to Brian, but I did. And I protected Mama from him during her grave illness.

A year ago, I found a missing piece of the puzzle. Brian was visiting cousin Sadie, and they talked about Mama. When I was ten and he was thirteen, Mama packed up her belongings and left us after her and Daddy's divorce was final. Brian was home, and Mama told him she was moving to another state. He started packing, but Mama told him he couldn't go with her. Mama told me a few years ago that Daddy would only give Mama a divorce if he gained custody of us kids. He knew Mama wanted us, but he didn't want to pay her child support.

Looking back, I think that after Mama had looked into Brian's eyes, his hurt and disappointment made her decide not to tell me she was leaving. Her baby and favorite, she couldn't look me in the eye. I accept that—I wouldn't be able to look into my own children's eyes and tell them that awful truth. Forty-five years later, I saw beyond her abandonment, and I let go of the hurt, healed, and moved forward.

Generational Wounding

It's amazing how a parent's actions can wound their children for a lifetime. But we need to look deeper and realize our parents carry their own wounds—generational wounds from their parents, and their parents' parents, on up through the familial line. These unhealed generational wounds are like curses that remain in the lineage until someone heals them.

I'd never heard of generational curses until a spiritual reader told me Erick and I had created a karmic situation during our affair that affects both of our family generational lines. These curses carry through multiple generations within the family and can involve sickness, inappropriate behavior, or repeating occurrences. My spiritual friend and fellow seeker, Astrid, says we're here to disrupt curses, transmute them, and change the course of our bloodlines. Here's an example of a generational curse that was created within my family.

Over several years, my great-grandfather and Grandpa disagreed about something and didn't speak to one another for several years. Later, when Mama divorced Daddy—without telling Grandpa that Daddy had abused her—Grandpa and my uncle showed up at the courthouse steps on the date of the divorce proceedings in hopes she would rescind her decision. They didn't change her mind. She divorced Daddy, and not being aware of the abuse, Grandpa didn't speak to her for five years. Grandpa just thought Mama had abandoned her children. Mama didn't ask for the abuse to be included in the divorce papers—she just wanted out of the marriage. When my great-grandfather passed away, Mama and Grandpa renewed their relationship without discussing their issues, and, despite their past disagreements, their relationship remained stable until his death. My uncle only realized all of this three years ago, after I shared the truth about the abuse with my aunt. Grandpa never knew the truth. Mama told me she didn't tell Grandpa intentionally because she knew Grandpa would've gone after Daddy and ended him.

After both my maternal grandparents died, Mama and her brother, my uncle, had a falling out involving an estate item. They both believed they were right—and I could see both sides of the dispute. Mama tried to make amends with my uncle, but he wouldn't allow it. Mama passed away, during COVID-19, without a resolution to their disagreement. He didn't even attend her celebration of life. Mama's generational curse of non-confrontation and allowing unhealthy family situations to happen and endure was passed down to me. Then the curse passed to my eldest son, Kurt. After I disclosed my affair with Erick, Kurt quit speaking to me. I'd held grudges, but through healing, grudges are a thing of the past for me. Kurt watched me do this for years, and now he's adopted my pattern. There's been no resolution, and Kurt hasn't forgiven me. So, it's the fifth generation for this curse within my family.

I thought about my estranged relationship with Kurt. After my divorce, I told my adult children about my affair with Erick because Erick's wife, Karen, had told their son about it. After the police charged her with harassment toward me, I feared that Karen would tell my sons about the affair, and I wanted them to hear it from me. Roman accepted the news, but Kurt turned his back on me. It has been six years since he's talked to me. I've reached out on holidays and his birthday, but there's never a response. I've tried. I'm at a loss, trying to accept that I have only one son in my life. I've prayed for Kurt to allow me back into his life, but there's been no change. I'm not bitter, just sad. He's angry, but still, friends and family can't believe he has turned his back on me. I sent him a painful text last year:

> *I'll always love you because you're my son, but if you don't reply, I won't continue sending texts. I've prayed for you to come back into my life. You weren't raised to be like this— without forgiveness. Parents aren't perfect... I'm an imperfect soul. If you decide to meet me halfway, I'll be overjoyed, but I'm walking away from your lack of empathy and selfishness.*
>
> *Life isn't perfect, and many times, it's unfair. People make mistakes. All I can do is what I continue to do... love you from afar. I hope you can forgive me. I'm sorry and regretful for the hurt and pain I caused you, Roman, and your dad. I'll always love you.*

I know curses are real, and I fear that my children, grandchildren, and beyond will suffer for my actions and continue the family curse. But I hope that by taking part in Ayahuasca ceremonies—and surrendering to Source—that the medicine will heal my family's curse before I leave this mortal coil. I realize that all our family members and all the family wounds remain unhealed and were buried with them after they died. I'd like to believe that when I die, all my children and grandchildren will get together and forgive all the family history of wounding, anger, and betrayal. As a Divine Feminine, I want peace in my bloodline and hope I'm doing enough in my remaining days to accomplish this.

The Sacred Feminine

Twin Flames are identified as the Divine Feminine and Divine Masculine. It isn't gender based but about the energy that lives in each of us (doing versus being, logical versus intuitive, aggressive versus loving, reason versus nurturing, firm versus gentle, etc.). Females can carry masculine energy, and males can be in their feminine energy. In today's world, which is influenced by masculine ideals and is a patriarchal society controlled by men, people have underestimated the value of the feminine and her wisdom and expression. Society has disrespected, silenced, and suppressed women for centuries. In past times, goddesses such as Athena, Aphrodite, and Isis were powerful. Women today are claiming our inner strength while embracing the goddess' signature energy.

The Divine or Sacred Feminine has light and dark energies. Some light feminine energy traits include our having strong intuition, healing ability, empathy, compassion, and patience. We're in touch with our emotions, we're receptive, and we forgive. However, our dark energy is misunderstood and reveals itself as passion, intensity, fury, fearlessness, power, strength, and sexual liberation. It isn't just about sex and sensuality, but as readers of my first book will remember, I understand now why, when I asked who I was during my second Ayahuasca journey, I heard clairaudiently, "Lilith."

Some people consider the dark female characteristics unfeminine or evil and mistake them for a shadow side and toxic femininity. But this isn't true. The Divine Feminine is an empowered, fierce, restored feminine essence, and for balance, we women should embrace both the dark and light within us. Sensuality is a powerful part of my Divine Feminine (which will make sense in the high-level channelings at the end of this book). Men I've had a strong connection with since my awakening have experienced no one like me. I'm gentle and kind while loving deeply and passionately.

There are seven feminine archetypes that embrace feminine energy, including Mother, Queen, Maiden, Sage, Huntress, Lover, and Mystic. I've identified with each of these at different points during my life. Each has made me a well-rounded Feminine.

Archetypes and Goddesses that represent the dark feminine are the Mesopotamian and Jewish Goddess Lilith and the Hindu goddess Kali Ma (or "Divine Mother"). Often, we deny the dark energy and are ashamed when perceived negative traits reveal themselves, but embracing these characteristics allows us to become our authentic selves. While many people reject the darkness and suppress it because of taboos, we in the Western world are embracing the "Goddess Movement." When you accept the dark Feminine's strength and power, it allows you to face your fears, and to grow and transform.

As I look back at my own choices and actions over the past seven years, I see I've encompassed both sides. Dark energy expresses sensuality and sexuality, but it goes beyond that. Light and dark energies conflict, but you don't have to pick one or the other—nor should you apologize or feel shame or guilt when walking a less-than-illuminated path. Balance both. Although I've walked in untamed darkness, those experiences allowed me to gravitate back to the light and purity within me. I don't apologize for my past actions because they were a necessary part of my journey to come full circle. Now my soul is gentle, my heart loves unconditionally, and my mind is clear.

Chapter Four

Discovering the Supernatural

Since childhood, I've had a fascination with the unexplained and the intervention of the Divine. For example, when my youngest son, Roman, was a baby, we were driving home when a fast-moving snowstorm happened. Twenty minutes from home, I felt a wave of terror as snow piled up in front of me. I made it up a steep hill in the treacherous conditions and was relieved. But then, two miles from home, the two-lane road curved on a slight incline. A vehicle was stranded in my lane, so I drove into the oncoming lane—but a vehicle was coming straight at me. I should've hit the car. With no time to react, I made it around the other car, avoiding a head-on collision. Over twenty years later, I know angels saved us.

I've been protected through the years. Twice when driving on the interstate, I was beside someone, close enough to where our side mirrors touched, but there was no resulting accident. This year, two drivers have almost hit my car on its front right fender at seventy miles per hour. I should've been hit. When I've realized the gravity of what could've happened to me, I've felt my angels around me. I've felt their coolness on my shoulders. It's inexplicable.

Another miracle happened once when I was climbing narrow rock steps at an Elohee retreat. I was high off the ground on the steps and lost my balance. I should've fallen. It felt like someone tugged my backpack and prevented me from falling.

Unexplained situations happen to me often. For example, at different times, one lady who worked with me in my home office saw and felt there was an entity with us. Within a week, I was upstairs in my home office, sitting in my chair, when I felt that something had its hand on my throat. It unnerved me. A month later at Christmas, I hired a medium (the medium who had first told me about Twin Flames) to come to our work Christmas party as an entertainer. I told her about the choking situation, so she went upstairs. She saw an adult male with a childlike demeanor (who'd been challenged mentally), who hadn't moved forward into the afterlife, as most souls do. She gave me advice and suggested I bring in a loving female energy to help him cross over. I was skeptical, but tried. I called upon Granny and her sister, Sadie's mother, to assist him, as they had always made me feel safe, and I knew anyone could feel comfortable with them. I assured the young man they were full of love and would support him. I pushed energy out of my body, hoping that would help, while visualizing them each taking one of his hands. *Will this work?* Two minutes later, my iMac had a loud power surge. I had an overwhelming sensation that the surge was their three energies leaving my home. After that, I didn't feel his energy again.

Our physical body can be the subject of supernatural experiences, too. After my lumpectomy and my mammogram were deemed normal, for example, my doctor wanted me to have a breast MRI and later told me there was a serious pocket of fluid in that area. Although there's some tenderness in the lumpectomy and lymph node removal area, normally I feel nothing else. A month after my MRI, one night, I couldn't sleep. It was like someone had touched that area. It wasn't painful but felt otherworldly. I had an intuitive thought that the Divine was working on and clearing the pocket of fluid. When I have my next breast MRI, I'll find out if the fluid is gone. Supernatural experiences are part of my journey, so I'm receptive to whatever Spirit offers me as intuitive hits.

Intuitive Hit

In my first book, I talked about when Daddy passed away. A month and day later, my ex-mother-in-law passed away. I was afraid I'd lose Sadie, who'd become my surrogate mom, a month and a day after that. My intuition niggled me. I'd done a Tarot reading about Erick, and the Death Tarot card had come up three days in a row. Two weeks later, I searched for Erick's mother's name on the Internet. She'd died on the same day that I'd been worried about losing Sadie. Knowing the love between them and how close Erick was to his mother triggered me. I felt pain for him.

That wasn't a coincidence.

Wanting to do something kind for Erick after he lost his mother, I looked for a sympathy card. Nothing I found in the store fit the situation. I used an online company to create a sympathy postcard. I sent him a text with a photo of a painting

I'd once commissioned, of a place where we could both retreat to in our minds when things were difficult. I chose a photo of the painting so he would know it was from me without me signing a card. (The painting became my first book cover). I mailed the postcard to his office, hoping he would receive it. The wording was:

> I'm sorry to hear of your beloved Mother's passing and pray for you during your time of loss. Know that I think of you, send wishes of healing, and understand the depth of love between Mother and son. Please remember the deep bond between the two is never broken, and her spirit remains a part of you no matter the time that passes or circumstances that occur.

Supernatural Events

While I was grieving for Erick's loss, another supernatural thing happened. One day, driving home, I took the back way through neighborhoods to avoid traffic. The route I took was near his mother's home. Granny was on my mind. Some traffic lights were functioning while others were flashing yellow, and they caused a delay. I saw a license plate with "Grandma" on it and another license that had the number 888 on it. 888 represents unconditional love. My Granny's energy surrounded me. Then, close to where Erick's mom lived, I saw Erick driving on the road in his truck. I sensed he saw me too, even with tinted windows in my car. It felt as though Granny played a part in us being brought together at that moment. A medium said Granny is working for my happiness on the other side.

Tapping into these supernatural events empowers my sensitivity and allows my intuition to expand. There have been countless times when I've acted on an intuitive nudge, only to find it's spot on. Once, something felt off about Erick, and I felt inspired to search local court records online. Erick had admitted to me that his drinking had precipitated his arrest several years ago for a DUI. After his and Karen's thirty-third wedding anniversary, the police had arrested him for domestic assault. There it was, in black and white: *State v. Erick Smith*. Karen was the witness, and Erick was the defendant.

I wept. Knowing Erick was in trouble and that he may have battered Karen hurt me. As a child who had witnessed domestic assault, I experienced a gamut of emotions, but I don't know the details. I questioned how I felt about it all. Erick isn't a perfect person, and I've never said he was. I'm not making excuses for his actions. His journey hasn't been easy. The charge was dismissed. I'm sure Erick has paid—in multiple ways. Karen now has this to hold over his head. But they haven't expunged the charge as they'd done with Karen's harassment against me, and I don't think they will because of the severity of the charge. When I called the court office and discovered Karen's expungement, it made me angry.

High Priestess Modalities

My supernatural experience and spiritual gifts inspire me to help others, so I want to start a spiritual business. There are forty different spiritual paths that interest me, but I don't want to be a jack of all trades and master of none. As a Virgo, we thrive when we do things well. A spiritual friend thinks I should start a YouTube channel or offer Tarot readings for people. Confidence in my Tarot abilities is growing, but I want to improve my skill set. (*That's my Virgo perfectionism in action.*) After writing my book and blogging about my journey, my top spiritual career choices are being a Tarot reader, a crystal/energy healer/cleanser, a pendulum dowser, and a psychic medium.

Tarot

I've listened to Tarot readings and read Tarot cards for almost seven years. Just as the cards attracted me, the pendulum has a similar energy, so I started using a pendulum to ask questions and receive answers. I have five pendulums made of different crystals: a purple amethyst, a clear quartz, a rose quartz, a moonstone, and an aquamarine crystal.

I use my aquamarine and rose quartz to gain insight on Erick. Just like the Crow Tarot deck, I use them to assess the energy of our Twin Flame connection, since we share a cosmic energy. Crows are a spirit animal for me, and I felt a strong connection to the deck in a short amount of time. Because one twin's energy reflects in the other twin's life (and vice versa), whenever I read about Erick and receive the Tower card, three of swords, or nine of swords, I brace myself. I know that means a challenge is happening in his life, which (because we're twin souls) will reflect on me. As I noted earlier, the week his mother passed away, the Death card came up three times. Death can mean changes and transformation, but in that case, the card represented actual physical death.

I own fifty Tarot and oracle decks and use a few decks consistently. Sometimes, friends ask me to check on their situations, and I do. To comprehend current energies, I lay out a card spread. As noted, because my Twin Flame's energy reflects on me, I check his energy sometimes, as it reveals situations that are coming into my energetic field. For those in my inner circle who request readings, I use specific decks. For my personal energy, I lay out the black and white Phantomwise Tarot deck. When I see the Tower card in a spread for Erick or me, I feel dread. I'm tired of having the rug pulled out from under me. The cards are accurate with messages they give me. Things that make little sense at the time will come to fruition later.

Crystals

Going to different crystal stores and perceiving the energetic vibrational frequencies of the stones, I'm comfortable in selecting and using the right stones for me. I'm drawn to crystals for healing and ones that help me connect to Divine through my third eye. Nirvana quartz, Libyan desert glass, K2, prophecy stone, triolite, and dumortierite have all helped me develop my psychic abilities. These stones also help facilitate my Ayahuasca visions.

I wear many crystals, and I've even slept with several stones. Because I've had nocturnal lagophthalmos since childhood (the inability of the eyes to close during sleep), I've slept for fifteen years with an eye mask, so my eyes are protected. The mask I use allows me to place stones under my mask, against my third eye. After a few months, I stopped placing the stones, but I know they helped me open my third eye.

At my favorite crystal store, I met a beautiful and angelic blonde lady, Mandi, who is a medical intuitive and medium. She always recommends the perfect stone for what my body and mind need and gives me explanations of how to use each one. Before radiation treatment, Mandi recommended a sugilite necklace. Sugilite is a healing stone and can eliminate negative energy during radiation. It offers spiritual protection, dreams, and purification and helps the wearer to become a "beacon of light."

I wear several spiritual beaded bracelets. One of my favorites is the sensual moonstone. I wore an overcoming heartache bracelet for years during my dark night of the soul. A sound bowl healer designed it and infused it with the sound from his musical bowls. Aventurine, rhodonite, and rose quartz combined help heal heartbreak, as does rhodochrosite. Many pieces I've bought have supported my healing. Use of crystals and stones quickly aids my recovery from triggers. When a bracelet's stone or elastic string breaks, it's usually a positive sign that I no longer need the bracelet, symbolizing transformation and completing a cycle. It can also show the crystal is protecting me from further harm.

Astrology

As I went deeper into spirituality, I reconnected with my connection to astrology, which I've been attracted to since childhood. It's another tool that reveals helpful information about a person's personality. However, not all people within the same astrological sign exhibit the same characteristics. Planet placement at a person's time of birth influences their characteristics. Because I resonate with astrology, I asked myself, "What would be a meaningful impression to symbolize who I am astrologically?" I gravitated toward having a tattoo—and I decided on black, as I love the simplicity without color. I'm a Virgo Sun and Moon sign, with Scorpio rising/ascendant. Most people don't share the same Sun and Moon sign. I found the images I wanted, and the day I turned fifty, I got my first two tattoos. As a double Virgo, I got a Virgo Sun sign tattooed on the outside of my right middle finger and the Virgo constellation behind my left ear. Without considering the pain level, I didn't realize that getting one behind my ear would hurt less than having one on my finger! The pain on the outer finger is intense, especially as the needle nears the palm. Still, I love my tattoos and have no regrets.

I wanted a new tattoo to celebrate the release of my first book. During the design process, I used the symbol for unconditional love throughout the book because I have unconditional love for my partners, family, and friends. I had it tattooed on my inner right wrist as a reminder of Erick and our Twin Flame journey. It's my favorite. When anyone asks me about it, I share my journey of unconditional love with them. It's a constant reminder of what I'm here to do… to teach, to heal, and to give unconditional love without expectation.

Chapter Five

Telling the Truth

After cancer, I'd increased the distance I walked on the greenway each morning. One morning, I saw an older lady using a walker while taking photos of the same white wildflowers I'd photographed a couple of days earlier. Her name was Ms. Zita, and we struck up a conversation. We had a good rapport. She used to be a runner in Phoenix, Arizona, and had moved to the area recently. She's twenty years older than me and reminds me of Granny. At 100 pounds, she's tiny and frail. Her biggest desire was to not be tied to her walker, so we started meeting in the early mornings on the greenway, where I offered to assist her walking one lap without the walker. I slowed my pace and always had my hand available for her unsteady moments. I believed she was brought in divinely for me to feel supported and less lonely. She's there for me emotionally and was non-judgmental as she learned about me.

In early August, while walking the greenway on a day when Ms. Zita wasn't available, I got a text from Jay, a guy from my high school whose name I recognized but whom I didn't know. He asked, "What year did you graduate?" I responded, "I graduated a year before your cousin." By the time we went back and forth several times through Messenger, an hour had passed.

I asked Jay if he still lived in our hometown—a thirty-minute drive from me—and found out he had a powerful government job in an adjoining state. Once I understood his role, I was in awe. We reminisced about our hometown, classmates, and teachers we knew.

Jay had had a tough childhood and a complicated and toxic relationship with his mother.

Each day, we texted, and our friendship blossomed quickly. Sometimes I heard from him often, but sometimes, he was busy with his career. It was nice to have a friendship with a man. He knew I was going out of town for a work conference and gave me his work account through Messenger because he wanted me to always be able to reach him.

Once I had Jay's other account, our communication increased. He liked my directness. We shared a similar sense of humor and had things in common. We flirted and sent each other social media reels. Jay came to our hometown every month or two, and I hoped to meet him. I was disappointed when I discovered he was in town working on his father's home but was too busy to meet with me. However, I figured we'd meet in time. On another weekend, he attended his class reunion, but again, we didn't meet. Jay mentioned he'd seen my first childhood friend, Marie, there.

Marie had been my childhood next-door neighbor and is in many of my earliest memories. She was my first friend. Her loving family was kind to me when I was small. Marie remembers Daddy's anger and was protective of me. I'm younger than her, but Marie, our siblings, and I were stair-steps in age, so we played together most days.

Jay drove into town a few more times, but he never had time to meet me. Still, we kept texting. Once, he sent me a picture of him taking a bubble bath. I sent a seductive photo of myself. *How could I be this attracted to someone I'd never met in person?*

Christmas was coming, and I knew Jay would be in town for several days. He expressed no interest in meeting, and that dashed my hopes of ever meeting him. Our texts slowed, then resumed. I shared news of my breast cancer when I was diagnosed.

Concerned, Jay supported me. In January, he asked, "Have you met anyone?"

"No."

"Have you met anyone?"

"No."

Our texts were still flirty but not as titillating in tone as before.

In February, close to the time for me to begin radiation, Marie reached out and wanted to take me for two of my radiation treatments. We hadn't spoken in a few years, but whenever we did, it was like no time had elapsed in our friendship. I look up to her. She has angelic energy. During our long phone call, she told me she'd met someone at a school reunion and was happy. I had a deep intuitive thought.

Was it Jay?

When Marie named Jay as who she met, I felt the room spinning. I thought I might vomit and ended the conversation.

Sleep escaped me for three days. Marie's friendship was important to me, and I didn't want to lose it. *If I tell her, will she hate me? Will she think I am trying to sabotage her relationship with Jay?* I talked to Samantha, my best friend, and a couple of other close friends, trying to decide what to do. Samantha and I have been friends for fifty years, and we go back to kindergarten. She's an intuitive Scorpio.

Consensus was that Marie would turn against me. Radiation started in just a few days, and I couldn't allow her to take me without telling her. If the truth ever came out, I'd feel I was being deceitful. My blood boiled at being placed in this situation. *I won't keep this to myself. It's not fair to Marie.*

Anxiety and guilt-ridden, I asked Marie to meet me for dinner before she was to take me to my first radiation treatment. I wanted her to have an out if she didn't want to drive me after knowing the truth. We reconnected at a steakhouse restaurant on a frigid Monday night in February. Marie has light blue eyes and blonde hair. She's beautiful inside and out—she's kind, and her heart is loving.

By the time we'd reached our teens, Marie and I were running in different crowds. She was always popular, and I was well-liked, but I was never a part of the "in-crowd." I understood why Jay would want to be with her, not me.

As we sat across from each other in our booth and reconnected, I couldn't reveal what I'd come to tell her. People were sitting around us, and I didn't want to hurt her. After eating, it was time to leave. After putting our coats on, I asked, "Can we talk more in my car?" Knocking down my fear, I began. "When you said you had met Jay, I must tell you, he was also texting me. We've never met, and he cares for you, not me."

Marie was blindsided. She asked to see the messages between Jay and I. She became engrossed in Jay's words and the similarities between them and his conversations with her. She thought I'd entertained him, that I was giving him excitement, but that it meant nothing to him. "He lacks empathy sometimes," she said. "He was using you for pleasure. It's not okay. His conduct and character should be above that because of his job," Marie said.

I couldn't believe she was mad at him, not me. I was still unsure if it would affect our fifty-year friendship. She assured me it wouldn't change anything between us. I've lost so many people along my journey in recent years, and I would've been sad if she'd turned against me.

I experienced many emotions: sadness, anxiety, hopelessness. It's hard to determine which was related to the upcoming cancer treatment and which was from knowing the truth about Jay and Marie. When I got home after dinner, I was angry. He'd lied to me. I texted Jay. "I talked to Marie. I'm glad for you."

Jay asked, "What do you mean?"

"That you and Marie are seeing each other," I replied. *You know what I mean... and you're busted.*

"I guess, kinda. Very long distance, obviously. She's a nice person."

"Yes, she is. You should've told me so I wouldn't have kept texting you."

"How are you doing?" Jay asked. "I've been meaning to check in on you. You can text me anytime. Been keeping you on the prayer line daily."

No, you're trying to diffuse the situation.

"What did she say?"

"She likes you."

"Ya think so? She said she did, but I wasn't sure."

I felt sucker punched.

The following day, he texted, "Good morning! I hope you have a great day."

Jerk!

Marie and I spoke the following day. She hadn't changed her mind about taking me to radiation. Unbeknownst to me, after reading the texts between Jay and me, after our conversation, she'd confronted him and told him to make it right.

When she and I talked on the way to treatment, we both thought our conversation had taken place a few weeks ago instead of two days earlier. Something inside felt like a timeline had shifted. This was a lesson for both of us.

The morning my radiation started, by way of trying to satisfy Marie's request for him to rectify this messed up situation, Jay sent this text:

> *I'm aware of what happened and I'm sad—I never meant to hurt your feelings. I've enjoyed our conversations. The situation with Marie was unexpected and we're figuring it out together. She knows I'm texting you. Don't worry about any texts or pics—I'd never share them and will delete everything to put your mind at ease. I hope you're okay and I'll continue to pray for you.*

In the end, I only wanted Marie's happiness. I was triggered and felt rejected. Plus, I was starting radiation and had to focus on my health. I feared losing a dear friend, but Marie was supportive. I'm filled with gratitude that she embraced my words without passing judgment. I won't forget my feelings when delivering the truth to her. She could've been cruel, but she was mad at him for his dishonesty, to her and to me.

After what happened, I retreated into my inner world for a brief time to heal my latest wounding. I'll no longer put someone I've never met on a pedestal. I spent more time with my family on weekends, which seemed to help, because there I'm loved.

Chapter Six

Walking into Round One

Someone I didn't write about in my first book (other than in one sentence), was a man named Larry, seven years younger than me. I'd seen him three times at family functions over a few years, but I didn't know him until right after Mama died. My cousin Sadie and I went to the funeral home for Mama's visitation, and then we went to a Mexican restaurant. Sadie invited Larry to join us.

A hard worker, kind, well liked, and easygoing, Larry was playful and funny. For almost twenty years, he'd been married to my distant cousin, Brittany. After their breakup, the family had remained close to Larry because Brittany, apparently selfish and uncaring, had hurt Larry. We all got along well. Larry is best friends with my cousin Ted. The three of us are a comedy trio. Larry's schoolboy ways are endearing.

Less than a month after Mama's death, Larry invited me to dinner. During this time, I was in my masculine energy and was adjusting to life without Mama, and not making my best decisions. We were drinking and ended up at my place.

He told me later he'd been thinking about me since leaving my place the next morning. He thought I was "down to earth." It was nice to be around someone I got along with. He always let me know how much he appreciated and respected me.

"Do I scare you or excite you?" I asked.

"Both, 70/30," Larry said. "I've never had great sex before."

"To me, great sex is animalistic and raw while the lovers are living in the moment," I told him. "It's different from making love."

Larry told me that during our intimacy the night before, my face had morphed as he'd looked at me. (Another lover has told me that, too). Larry said he'd struggled to look me in the eye. When I'm involved with someone, I look deep into their eyes. A friend said my gaze can feel as though I'm looking into your soul. Larry said he'd sensed I was different. *He'd recognized my Divine Feminine.*

"Don't you think couples should be married before having sex?" Larry asked.

"It doesn't always work out like that," I replied.

Larry let me know he'd never been with a woman whose sex drive was as high as mine. I was bold with what I said and did with him, and he thought I was awesome, beautiful, and a perfect lady. He worried about satisfying me. Larry let me know by text when he was thinking of me. He liked when we cuddled, told me he wanted to enjoy me and my body, and said our honest, raw conversations blew his mind. We saw each other casually, but we weren't in a committed relationship.

Needing to leave town for a while, I booked a week-long beach trip for October and invited Sadie and her family, plus Larry, to come. We all had so much fun. Ted, Larry, and I kept the comedy going. Larry and I stayed high a large amount of the time, and we connected. In my intimate moment with Larry, I said what I wanted and needed, without shame. The week was amazing. Everyone agreed it was the best family vacation ever!

As our time together increased, I liked Larry more and more. Of course, Erick still had my heart, which was unfair to Larry. I struggled with Larry being younger than me, but it didn't seem to bother him. Larry thought I looked younger than my age. But when I found out he'd asked my cousins if they thought I was pretty, it hurt my feelings. Larry is the type of guy that needs others' approval.

"You're attracted to me or you're not," I told him.

Larry's ex-wife is twelve years younger than me, with average looks. Our family told me Larry thought she was beautiful— and knowing that contributed to my doubt and low self-worth.

Still, we hung out more, and things were going well. One afternoon, I invited Larry to come over after Samantha's Halloween wedding. He'd been drinking, but I thought he'd agreed to come. He didn't show up, and after I returned home that night, I texted him. He'd been at a NASCAR race. Confused, I told him, "You hurt my feelings."

In retrospect, he'd mentioned the race when we'd talked on the phone earlier, but I thought he'd still see me that night. I apologized, and he said, "You did nothing wrong."

"Why haven't we seen each other?" I asked.

"Because I respect you more!"

"Can't you respect me *and* sleep with me?"

"I'm trying," he said.

"I thought you were coming over."

"I don't want to see you as a whore."

I was devastated. Only one person had ever called me that: Karen, Erick's wife.

"I see," was all I could muster as a response. I stopped answering Larry's texts. I cried non-stop. He'd been verbally cruel to me.

Stewing, knowing Larry and I would both be attending a bonfire at Ted's, I prepared what I'd say. My anger had hit the boiling point, and he was going to get a taste of it. We were both outside at Ted's with no one around, so I waited until he finished a call and then I blasted him like I've never done before. If you've ever gone into a blind rage, you'll acknowledge what happened next.

Shaking, I went off on Larry, taking my hurt and dumping it on him. I stabbed my index finger into his chest repeatedly. My words were daggers. Neither of us likes conflict, but I had no problem with it right then. After spewing my anger, I retreated to the bonfire.

Larry wanted me to take an ATV ride with him. I'd calmed down, but I hesitated. I went. It was cold and dark as we rode. He turned the ATV off onto a gravel road and made amends with me. It turns out he'd been drinking heavily and had no recollection of the verbal pain he'd inflicted on me.

"It would be easy to fall in love with you," he said.

"Then kiss me."

It was a tender kiss. It felt like we'd turned a corner. I let forgiveness fill my heart.

However, Larry communicated less. Sadie said she thought it was because Larry was fearful after he and Brittany divorced. So, I treated him gently.

Family Christmas

COVID-19 had taken over most of the family that Christmas. As a family, we celebrated Christmas on New Year's Day. It was the day after I'd seen Erick at The Corner Cafe restaurant.

Those of you who have read my first book will recall that I'd been traumatized by the fact that Erick wouldn't look me in the eye when he told me he didn't love me anymore. It was all I could do right then not to sob. After that, I didn't want to be alone, so I was grateful to get together with my family. I was feeling pretty vulnerable at that point.

After our Christmas together, Larry helped me carry bags out to my vehicle. "Can you come over?" I asked him. "I need a friend."

He wouldn't come.

I went home alone and licked my wounds. *I shouldn't let others treat me this way.* I texted, "I can be friends with you or more than friends... I can't be friends with benefits. You're special, and I miss hanging out and texting." We talked that night, and Larry told me he was coming over the next day.

He never showed up. I was hurt.

I'd been needing some beach time, and had paid for a condo rental. Before Christmas, I'd invited my family along and I'd also invited Larry. Anger came over me. There was no way I was going if Larry was going to be there.

"Try to forgive Larry," Sadie said.

"I can't."

Lowering the boom, I texted:

When I asked you to the beach, I thought we were okay. You led me on—asking, "How do you know I don't feel the same?" and saying you'd call Sunday. You never called. When I confronted you on New Year's Day, you just snickered. I said I could use a friend, but you haven't reached out to check on me. That's not how friends act. I'm not comfortable vacationing together since we clearly aren't friends. Your apology seemed sincere, but your actions say otherwise.

Larry asked, "What are your expectations of me? You cut me out of all the family texts."

"Expectations?" I replied. "There's none after New Year's Day. That's why I chose to not include you in future texts. You need to think about how your actions caused this." All of this caused hurt within my family. Because they love us both and didn't want to take sides, my family chose not to come. Roman, some friends, and I went instead. The weather was amazing that week, so we had a wonderful trip. After returning, I dreaded knowing I would see Larry soon on the next family holiday.

Holiday Gatherings

The gravity of this situation weighed on me. At Easter, when Larry came out to my vehicle to carry dishes, I was still angry and hurt, so I was cold to him. My boundaries were in place, and my walls were up.

Then, on the Fourth of July, we had another family gathering. I avoided making eye contact throughout the afternoon. He's a water sign and intuitive (most of them are). I didn't want to speak to him, and I pushed that energy out to him. He stayed away from me.

When I got home after seeing him at the family Thanksgiving lunch, I texted him, wanting to make amends. A few months went by, and I was no longer mad at Larry. "I wanted to speak with you alone and didn't get to today. I want to make peace between us. I've been hurt and angry, but I don't want any bad feelings between us anymore. Would it be okay to move forward?"

Larry texted back to say he'd wished I'd talked to him. "I'd love to talk and hang out again," he said. "I know you're a good person, and there are no hard feelings. I wanted to talk to you today as well."

At our family Christmas dinner, we started talking in person again. It could've been awkward, but it wasn't. Then, within a week, the doctors had diagnosed me with cancer.

Larry texted me after my diagnosis, and I sensed his kindness.

"I hated hearing the unfortunate news about your breast cancer. I wish there was something I could do to take it away. You'll be in my prayers. If there's anything I can do, please call and let me know. I have faith that the good Lord will get you through this. Love you very much and please stay in contact." Gratitude filled my heart because Larry didn't have to be supportive of me, but he was.

There were life-size dummies in my oncology office. One looked like a life-sized Cabbage Patch doll. I did funny things with them while I was in the office. Happily, I kept my sense of humor throughout the disease. One day, I sat on a dummy's lap (with my arm around its neck), took selfie photos, and shared it with my family's group text thread. Our group texts let everyone know I was doing well, and everyone sent me support. I appreciated their kind sentiments and prayers, and Larry's concern mattered to me—a lot.

Larry and I were friendly again. Our family went to the beach the following summer. Knowing things might still be uncomfortable between us, I guarded myself. Larry did funny things, and I couldn't help but laugh at him. He doesn't mind being the butt of jokes. Larry and I went to see an Elvis movie, and we shared a THC vape pen before going into the theater. We enjoyed getting high together, and we spent late nights smoking on the condo balcony. When high, Larry is superficial, while I go deep within.

While we were sitting out on the balcony, Larry admitted, "I was envious of that dummy, you know. And I was sad when I found out you were dating the guy who was a preacher."

After he said that, it started up between us again, and we fooled around. I leaned down to him, grasped his chair handles, leaned over him, looked into his eyes, and said something sensual to him. But we respected our family, and that meant no sex during our trip.

Because I'd never apologized in person, I wanted to look at him and tell him I was sorry. I told him, "When I yelled at you that night two years ago? I've never done anything like that before. I was hurt. Later, you weren't honest with me, and I lashed out. I'm sorry I said what I did and the way I acted. Do you forgive me?"

Larry said, "I forgave you a long time ago. I want us to be on the same page and not mislead you."

"Do you want us to be in the friends-only zone?" I asked.

"I haven't thought about that," he said.

"Friends don't do what we did on the balcony."

"I enjoy being around you," he said. "I'd tell you if I didn't care for you. I can't remember the last time I wanted to hang out with someone."

We started talking and texting again.

Chapter Seven

Connecting in Sedona

Six months after the radiation ended, I was moving forward with life. After months of planning, I traveled and met other seekers at a ladies' retreat in Sedona, one of the top spiritual hubs in the United States. Many of us had met at the Dragonfly retreat at Elohee Retreat Center in North Georgia a year earlier. Elohee is a tranquil oasis of self-discovery, growth, and holistic wellness. It's on top of a mountain, where the Cherokee people lived in generations past. I've been to several Dragonfly retreats at Elohee, which led to my healing path. While on the land,

I feel safe. There's a 100-foot waterfall that brings me peace. (If you ever get the chance to attend, I highly recommend it (elohee.org)). The ladies and I traveled to Cottonwood, Arizona, where we stayed for a week in a boutique hotel. We were ecstatic to be reunited. Each of us knew that this retreat would differ from what Elohee had offered in the past.

The huge cacti and the desert mountains, with their varying shades of clay, mesmerized me. The heat differed from home, and, hoping I wouldn't burn in the September sunshine, I brought sunscreen along. On the first full day, we had free time. We went to the Tlaquepaque Arts and Crafts Village, a shopping center in Sedona, and visited a crystal store. I wanted to purchase something special and was excited to find a meteorite flower-of-life pendant.

On Tuesday, our group went to Bell Rock and the Chapel of the Holy Cross, which is on the National Register of Historic Places. As we drove up the winding road, I was excited. Part of the Chapel of the Holy Cross was enclosed within the rocky, red rock mountain cliff. Marguerite Brunswig Staude, a rancher and sculptor, had inspired and commissioned the Chapel. She completed her vision in 1956, and it's now part of the Roman Catholic Diocese of Phoenix. It's a beautiful place for prayer and reflection.

When I walked inside, I was in awe—it's a spiritual, holy place. There was bench seating with red cushions, and I sat down. Looking up at the ninety-foot iron cross of the crucified Jesus was overwhelming. From that holy place, I sensed Jesus' compassion differently than I ever had—I felt Jesus' love for me. His eyes followed me throughout the chapel. I moved onto the cushioned prayer kneeler and wept and prayed. As I looked up at our Lord and Savior, I felt unworthy of the gift I'd been given: *His ultimate sacrifice.* I wanted to remove the crown of thorns from his head. Not wanting to leave, I stayed longer than most of my companions. When I saw the thick nails hammered into His hands, I felt helpless. I stared at the casts of his feet and lit a candle before leaving. Over two years later, the visit still affects me. For whatever reason, I had a deep connection to Jesus that day.

We went to Airport Mesa for a nice dinner. After we ate, it was time to watch the beautiful Sedona sunset. Rays of light were beaming from the clouds in the sky. I time-lapsed a video of the sun in a brilliant collage of reds and oranges as it emerged from behind the distant mountains.

Temperatures exceeded 100 degrees most days. We were excited to go for a hike, where we had views of Cathedral Rock. The multi-colored rock was amazing—but I made sure I kept my eye on the ground, watching for snakes and creepy crawlies. At one of Sedona's vortices, which is part of Cathedral Rock, we met a man named Robert, who hands out hand-carved heart-shaped rocks to hikers. According to him, the rock he gave each of us embodies the energy of the vortex and represents unconditional love. Sedona vortexes are thought to be swirling centers of energy that assist in healing, meditation, and self-exploration

The following day, we went on a Mystical Tour to Rachel's Knoll, which requires driving through a gated homeowners' area. It's on the top of a mountain, at one of Sedona's seven vortices. You can feel the energy swirl. According to the plaque at the Knoll, Rachel Petty Lunt was a remarkable woman who worked hard to gain and preserve the property. We sat on yoga mats while meditating and connecting with the land. I was at peace, looking out at the distant mountains. I embraced my feminine power.

It was time to go to Amitabha Stupa and Peace Park, a sanctuary for people from all walks of life, to sit, pray, and meditate. We each walked around the stupa quietly. There were four prayer wheels filled with sacred mantras and prayers for peace. They've stamped the mantra of universal compassion into the wheels. When you walk around them in a clockwise direction, virtuous energy goes out to the world. I sat and meditated in front of a tall, mahogany Shakyamuni Buddha statue. As a group, we meditated in the park.

On Thursday, we went for a hike at Buddha Beach, another area of vortex energy. At the beginning of our hike, I saw Cathedral Rock from a fresh vantage point. When I saw the two small rocky areas between the larger mountains, they looked like a masculine and feminine rock formations embracing each other. I was drawn to this area—and I saw more grass there than anywhere I've been in Arizona. We walked along a river where small white flowers were blooming.

On the hike, we stood by a large tree and grounded ourselves. I sat on the clay and meditated and prayed. Columns of stacked rocks in the area seemed to balance on top of one another, defying gravity, not tipping over because of the vortex of energy. We stayed a long time at the beach. We walked through the river to get to a large rock, and we sat on it for an hour, blown away by the beauty and tranquility of the place. As we returned to our van, I sensed Erick's energy. I saw my spirit animal, a crow, cawing, seemingly at me. At that moment, I felt connected to Spirit. Of the places we had visited, the beach and chapel were my favorites.

Our last day arrived, and we went to the Boynton Canyon Trail in the Coconino National Forest. There were a few colored hot air balloons floating over the area. I'd released my book three weeks earlier, so I had an official book release event in the canyon and gifted each person with a book. Of all the places I could've held my book launch, this was the most spiritual place for it to happen. The photos we took were amazing, with the red mountains in the background. We all stayed and enjoyed the view.

Later that day, the three of us had psychic readings at the Tlaquepaque Arts and Shopping Village. The information the psychic gave me about Erick wasn't what I wanted to hear, although I knew in my heart it to be true: *He's not coming back.* The reading triggered me, and I couldn't stop crying. *When am I ever going to accept he has free will and is choosing to remain in his marriage?* It's a hard pill to swallow. At the end of the reading, the psychic told me someone would come into my life in the next few weeks. *Could it be Larry wanting to rekindle our relationship?*

Because I was upset, I declined to attend a steak dinner in Cottonwood. For our final gathering, the ladies surprised me with a card and a large piece of chocolate cake to celebrate my birthday and the book release. Through tears, I blew out my candle and wished for happiness to come my way.

Sedona had offered me so much. Sometimes, when people are finding their spiritual path, they move there, and I can understand why.

Back at home, it was time to promote my book. I'd lacked the knowledge of what I needed to do to publish a book (beyond writing my manuscript), so I engaged the services of the boutique publishing company PRESStinely to work with me to release it. I didn't include my photo in the book—I still wanted to remain hidden.

Secretly, I hoped Erick might read my words. I hoped our story might bring him back. Although I can't be sure, I think he's aware of it and may have read it because of a clairvoyant vision I had. In the vision, I couldn't see any faces, but I could hear two men talking. One was sitting behind a desk. One man mentioned my name, pulled a desk drawer open, and gave a book to the other man.

PRESStinely encouraged me to do podcasts and a blog, but I didn't want the public to see me. I'm not a natural speaker—I stumble over my words and get anxious. But, after the release of my book, I gathered my courage, and took part in seven podcasts. Though my nerves are what they are, I did well with sharing information about being a Twin Flame and my journey. All the podcasters put me at ease. I told each of the podcasters I'd answer questions except ones about my Twin Flame. I wanted to respect his family's privacy. I carefully chose my responses when I answered questions, so Erick was protected.

Two days after my return from Sedona, I had a podcast scheduled. After having had the upsetting psychic reading, I was hesitant about the podcast because I felt vulnerable. Although I tried to be strong, the host asked me a question that made me cry. I composed myself and finished the podcast. *When will I reach a point where talking about Erick won't trigger me to cry?*

That Sedona-reading trigger lasted two weeks. I'm so tired of darkness overcoming me and gloominess remaining when the triggers happen. *What else must I learn, and when will I move on from the lessons I signed on for during this lifetime?* I know part of my mission here is to help others understand the Twin Flame experience, so I pray I learn these lessons well so I can help you work on healing, too. If you're interested, my podcasts and blog are on my website: healingsacredwounds.com.

Chapter Eight

Falling into Round Two

A couple of weeks went by after I returned from Sedona, and things were friendly and respectful with Larry, but he hadn't asked me out. *Could the psychic have been wrong?* I shared my frustration with the situation with my cousin Ted and asked for his advice.

"Tell Larry," Ted said.

Next time Larry and I texted, I said,

In Florida, you said you wanted us to go out. If you're not interested in more than friendship, tell me. I'm done with maybes and this middle school dynamic. If you were interested, we'd have progressed by now. It might hurt, but I'd rather know where we stand. I want someone in my life regularly, and that's not too much to ask.

Larry texted, "Now isn't the best time for me to be talking about this with you. I've had a few beers and don't want to say something wrong. But there are things I'd like to talk to you about."

He didn't want to say anything he might regret, like before. I tried to reassure him.

Larry said, "I thought we were perfect together. I found that out in Florida."

"I did, too."

He added, "I understand that. I enjoy being with you, too. I don't want to make a wrong move. You mean that much to me, that's why. Whatever happens will happen. I don't want to lead you through any false pretense."

Larry told me he cherished our time together and saw me as honest and beautiful. He wanted us to meet for dinner at a seafood restaurant. Larry was concerned about us seeing each other again. He asked, "What if the situation doesn't work out between us?"

When I'm seriously interested in someone, I never think about the situation not working out. My heart leads me emotionally, and negative thought patterns are non-existent. I can't imagine Larry not being a part of my life and hoped it would be romantically.

At the restaurant, I said, "If it doesn't work out, we can stay friends." It's what he needed to hear. I was ready for things to be physical again between us. It'd been a long time since I'd been intimate with anyone.

We went back to my place after dinner, and I dropped clothing, piece by piece, walking to my bedroom, with him behind me. Larry was the only man who had seen me heavier, before my mommy makeover. Now, after my surgery and lumpectomy, he saw me with scars—and I was smaller. After we reconnected physically, I lay on my back, and he lay on top of me, his back against my chest. I wrapped my arms and legs around him like a spider. He said he liked how it made him feel. It was good to be close to him and have a connection. *The psychic was right.*

Peace and Healing

Things were going well. I was in a period of reflection following my cancer journey, and I wanted closure. Luke (a former priest I'd been involved with) came back into my life. I met him for an early dinner on the afternoon of my last radiation treatment. He clasped my left hand across the dark wood table and told me he could be there to help me spiritually or romantically, but that he wanted to marry me. I was wearing Granny's pink ice ring on my left ring finger. He said it could be replaced with a diamond. I let those words absorb but didn't give him a response.

Luke's statement sparked a memory in me. I remembered Erick picking up my Levian strawberry gold, sapphire ring and pushing it on his ring finger until it stopped near his knuckle, as if he was sizing it. This was around the time Erick had said he wanted to marry me.

I won't marry again if Erick remains in my psyche.

During dinner, Luke asked me to meet him over the weekend at a hotel four hours away. I sensed his desire for me and knew he wanted to be intimate. That wasn't on my radar. I was exhausted from cancer treatment, and I declined. I didn't have the strength to drive to the hotel. Also, I wasn't ready for Luke to see three fresh scars from my lumpectomy site, lymph node removal, and catheter insertion. I was vulnerable. Many thoughts went through my mind, and I felt that what he'd asked was presumptuous and inconsiderate. Luke took it all personally and ghosted me again. I sensed his rejection wound.

After I released *My Twin Flame Journey*, I wanted peace and healing between Luke and me. So, seven months later, in November, I reached out to him again. I thought he might be able to help me interpret my Ayahuasca visions. Sitting there, I remembered that right after Luke and I'd first been intimate, nearly two years earlier, I'd had a vision of a sacred geometric shape. It had started as what I can only describe as a nautilus shell, then expanded until it looked like a DNA double-spiral helix.

"Good to hear from you," Luke said. "I'd be happy to help you. Tell me what the medicine gave you."

I told him:

I felt guided and saw ancient codes I can't draw or fully understand. Through my opened third eye, I've seen that I'm meant to heal others, but I must heal from cancer first. You appear in my spiritual journeys, and I need your guidance that others can't provide. I'm being elevated and received the message that I'm chosen. During Reiki cleansing, I saw Jesus' crown of thorns and heard "She's ready" with God's energy before me and Jesus behind me.

"That's amazing," Luke said. "How are you feeling? I hope and pray your medical follow-ups have gone well."

"I'm doing well. I've been living my life to the fullest by going on trips and delving deeper into spirituality. In early July, I go back for another mammogram. If that one is clear, there's one last six-month mammogram in January, and then I'll have yearly ones."

"My father was diagnosed with a lung tumor last week," Luke said. "The doctors were presenting him with treatment options, but his condition wasn't good. He wasn't sure if he wants to fight this, but seems at peace with it."

I was sad to hear Luke's news.

When we said goodbye, things were calm between us.

A Happy Fall

After reflecting on my closure with Luke, I enjoyed the lovely fall season. Larry and I got together once a week, although I wanted to see him more. Samantha met him and surprised me when she said, "Larry and Erick resemble each other."

What?! After she brought it to my attention, I could see the physical similarities with their coloring, size, and facial features, although Larry is three inches taller. Larry and Erick share the same astrological sign, although Erick is fifteen years older than Larry.

Larry and I enjoyed our dates. One night, we were in my bed for three hours talking and growing closer without intimacy. We went to the lake at night sometimes. We were parked at the shoreline, sitting and talking in the front seat, gazing out peacefully at the lake. We both loved being there. It was late, and I ended up in his lap, kissing him. I lay on the horn accidentally. After we stopped laughing, I became putty in his hands. We drove home and hung out. As he was leaving, I walked with him to the door. At the bottom of my stairs, he spun me around. I grabbed the newel post, and he handled me in a way that brought me alive. He seemed to understand my Divine Feminine sensuality, which is what I wanted... and needed.

Larry tries to act confident, but I read through his smoke screen. He doesn't have much experience with women. "I get nervous around women, but not you," he said. Larry has anxiety, and he expresses his childhood trauma in different ways. With my wounding, thoughts, and actions, I understand him better than most people do. He's a gentle clean freak and would help anyone who needs it. I told Larry I wasn't sure whose childhood was more messed up, his or mine.

Our family thinks Larry and I are alike, and that we're perfect for each other. When Ted sometimes chides Larry too much, I feel bad. But he's quick-witted and seems to handle it better than most people—he can laugh at himself. Larry complimented the podcasts I took part in for the release of *My Twin Flame Journey*. "I'm proud of you," he told me.

I was preparing for my upcoming Ayahuasca retreat. Knowing I was supposed to abstain from drinking, THC, and intimacy for three weeks before going, Larry teased me sexually. *So this is how it's going to be?*

Sensuality is a large part of who I am, and I don't shy away from it. I embrace it. I went to my bathroom, put lingerie on, and asked him to come into the bedroom to help me with something. I still smile when I remember the look on his face. I brought my A game. *Ummm... two weeks clean.*

Things were going well between us. I'd learned to be in the moment with Larry and wasn't thinking of Erick as often. In bed, I was telling him about my recent trip to Ayahuasca when I knew—*I've fallen in love with Larry.* After I shared my Ayahuasca experience, I hinted that there was something I'd realized.

"Say it."

I looked him in the eye and said, "I love you." I hoped he'd return the sentiment.

"Thank you," he said.

What? My feelings were hurt. I'd been vulnerable. I didn't feel rejected, but it was a blow to my ego.

Larry hadn't been to a popular tourist area in several years. I asked him if he wanted to go on a quick weekend trip to the mountains, and he agreed. After his divorce, he'd lived with his Mom, Bonnie, who suffered from diabetes. How a man treats his mother speaks volumes, and Larry is good to Bonnie.

Before we went out of town, Larry was worried about Bonnie's health, but she insisted we have fun. As we made our way to the mountains in early December, we talked non-stop for four hours. It was a relaxing and fun time. We enjoyed different restaurants, and I looked forward to seeing the holiday lights. It was an enjoyable, stress-free weekend.

Before we headed home, Larry spoke with Bonnie. He was dreading going home. On the drive home, we were quiet. Trying to calm him, I said, "It'll be okay." But when he got home, Bonnie was admitted to the hospital for a diabetic foot wound. Larry was managing her care while taking care of the family business. He was going back and forth between the hospital and home. I didn't see him for three weeks but gave him my support. Thankfully, Bonnie returned home before Christmas.

Knowing Larry didn't like anyone showing up unannounced, I called him on a cold Christmas Eve and told him I'd cooked a meal for him and Bonnie. I think he was embarrassed because he lives with his mom, though he loves and takes care of her. Surprisingly, he said, "Come over." He greeted me at the front door. I hadn't planned on staying, but he invited me to ride along with him as he ran a few errands. In the Explorer, he put his hand in my lap, smiled, and seemed happy I was there.

Before New Year's, Bonnie returned to the hospital, incoherent. Larry was worried about her—I was, too. She required a rehab stay. When Bonnie's health improved, the first time Larry had free time, he went out with his friends—two nights in a row. That hurt and irritated me. *If he cares about me, shouldn't he want to spend time with me when the time comes available?*

Wrong.

I texted him:

In the mountains, I enjoyed our time together. When I opened up in bed and said "I love you," you just said "Thank you." I felt foolish. You called me pretty "in a schoolteacher way"—

what does that mean? Your ex-wife is a schoolteacher. When I tell you that you turn me on, you say nothing. I want and need intimacy. You're a good person and loving son. I've given you space and been there for you, but sports and friends always seem to come first. We aren't on the same page, and it saddens me. I don't want to be a "Waitie Katie"—I want someone who chooses me.

My love languages are quality time, words of affirmation, and physical touch, but I'm not receiving any of that. Our needs are different. I'm giving without getting much back. I love you unconditionally, which is why I'm not mad. I'll still be here as a friend when you reach out.

Larry responded, "I'm not used to being with someone that likes and expects what you do… I'm hearing you in the text. We'll talk about it when we talk. Anyway, I wanted to let you know that I've seen the text."

Upset, I called him.

"I'm angry and upset over what you said," Larry told me.

We discussed how each of us felt about what had transpired. I hoped for it to be a disagreement, but I think it went deeper than that for Larry. Looking back, I questioned if his abandonment and rejection wounds were activated. I hoped he'd understand my point of view, but we were at a stalemate.

Through tears, I said, "It can't always be lollipops and gumdrops."

At the end of our conversation, I hoped we'd be okay.

Chapter Nine

Reading From a Spiritual Discerner

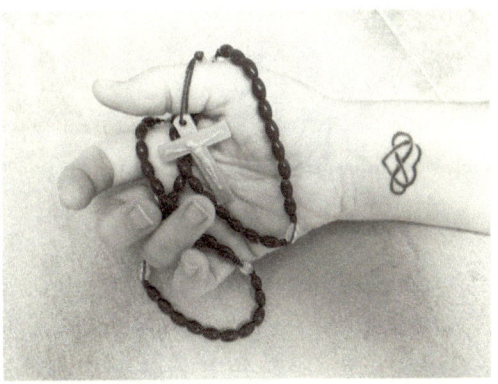

After the breakup with Larry, I knew I had to heal more. I searched and found a silent retreat five hours away in a rural location. I'm talkative, and this would be a challenge for me, but I was determined to adhere to the no-talk rule. This retreat required that each participant cook one healthy meal. I cooked a low-fat, homemade turkey meatball spaghetti.

Realizing this wasn't Elohee, I made the most of my time. *I will try to heal from Larry and release Erick more.* We all stayed in tiny cabins, and I loved mine—it was named Peace. Each evening, we had discussion time, and one night, one man talked about building a home constantly. *Can't he just shut up?* I started crying because his reason (and others) for being there seemed superficial and mine was deeper than that. Though my tears turned off several participants, I stayed with feeling my pain body (a concept introduced by author and spiritual mentor Eckhart Tolle). It's caused by painful life experiences that weren't accepted or faced when they happened, and describes amassing repressed emotions that live within us. At that moment, I felt alone and wanted to leave. Well, you get what you pay for, and not all retreats have the same quality. I won't be returning. My hopes of healing there were dashed. Back to reality and the aftermath of Larry and my breakup.

A wave of sadness washed over me as time passed, and Larry didn't express interest in reconciliation or have contact with me. The first time I saw him after our split was two months later at a Mexican restaurant, where we caught glimpses of each other. When Larry walked out to his vehicle, I was leaving, and I drove over to him and told him I missed him. He said he missed me but was guarded in talking to me. Looking back, I realize our breakup had exposed Larry's wounds.

Sadie told me later that at church, over a period of a few weeks, Larry had kept asking about me. I thought he might come to his senses, and we'd return to each other, as I was willing to meet him in the middle. But it never happened.

Readings

I want to always be aware of what's going on in my life, and I seek psychic readings. I first consulted a psychic when I was eighteen. She told me about the two boys I'd have (and I did), and she told me I'd have a career in healthcare (which I do).

Over the past six years, I've had readings with five psychic mediums, and of course, there's no way they knew about the truths they delivered prior to those readings.

Trying to focus on my spirituality and not on Larry, I visited a local medium. In the last six years, I've visited or had sessions with a few mediums for clarity on several things. All mediums are psychic, but not all psychics are mediums. When they give me a reading (without knowing me), and they know my secrets, I'm always in awe. Of course, some mediums are more gifted than others. Since being told that I'm a favorite among my angel team and that I'll channel more in the future, I don't want to disappoint Divine. As my channeling increases, one day, I hope to offer mediumship and share my spiritual gifts.

I scheduled an appointment with one local seer, Mary, who considers herself a Spiritual Discerner of two faiths (a person who can tell the difference between types of spirits). Mary's family background includes a parent from both faiths, and she believes that her gift is from Jesus. She looked inside my soul. Mary doesn't consider herself a medium. She describes what comes to her. She sees spirits, and it's as if you're at a bar with her, and various people walk up and say something to her that's a message for you. In a subsequent reading, she mentioned a man named Dick and "the rosary." I knew it was Luke's dad she was speaking about. "He doesn't have long," she said. My deceased former brother-in-law also came through and told Mary about my affair with Erick. (He's still ill-natured in the afterlife!) Mary named his daughter and granddaughter and said he wanted me to tell them he loved them. (I didn't do it though, because my ex-niece is religious and doesn't believe in supernatural experiences.) At the end of our session, Mary gave me a blessed maroon and tan rosary. I keep it on my nightstand and use it during energetic healings.

Should I contact Luke about his dad?

I've received accurate messages from psychics and mediums about Mama, Daddy, and my favorite grandparents. Granny was a simple woman, but wise. I know that most of my spiritual gifts come from her lineage. However, through one mediumship reading, I discovered Grandpa had a spiritual connection, too. He also shared a telepathic connection with his identical twin. The medium who gave me that reading knew about a box I have that belonged to Grandpa.

My grandparents were my safety net, and several mediums have confirmed that they continue to surround me. So it turns out I'm not alone! Deb, one of my favorite psychic mediums, said, "Your deceased grandfather travels with you in your car." That might explain why I've been protected from accidents. Sometimes when I'm in my chair at home, I catch a flash of light out of the corner of my left eye and know that a presence is with me. I don't know if it's Grandpa, but I find it comforting.

These mediumship readings are healing. Most of the messages are profound, and they all hit close to home.

The discerner I saw said Daddy, in the spirit world, was desperate for me to forgive him. Another medium told me the same thing. I forgave Daddy three years ago, but now I understand that I hadn't released the pain. A medium told me Daddy has been in a life review since his passing. A life review is where a soul, after they die, watches their life experiences, including the things they've done wrong. Daddy has to watch what he did to Mama, Brian, and me over and over and see how it has affected each of our immediate family members. For his soul to learn, he has to experience the consequences of his actions. I asked God during my last Ayahuasca journey to allow him to be released from the review. That's why I've healed that wound. No one explained to me that releasing pain is part of forgiveness. Because of this, my pain remained longer than it should've. Forgiveness doesn't come with a rule book. I hope you're able to forgive those who have wounded you and release the pain.

The mediumship readings I've had are important to my spiritual growth. I decided that I'd study to be a medium myself and began a mediumship program. As my gifts increase,

I'm no longer afraid of what's coming into my life. Others might consider my path unconventional or think that these gifts aren't from God. But I know angels surround and protect me. For whatever reason, it's all needed as we ascend to the New Earth. My gifts are developing, and my knowledge is increasing. I want to use those gifts to assist people in whatever way I can, while in service to God.

After contemplating what the discerner had told me about Luke's father, I reached out to him. "I saw a Spiritual discerner earlier this week," I said. "Your dad's name came through. Would you like to know what the discerner said?"

Luke replied, "Yes."

"I was told he doesn't have long to live."

Luke asked, "Did she say how long he has? We're trying to figure out if it's a few weeks or a few months."

"It feels like a shorter time to me," I said. "I knew it was your dad she spoke of because 'rosary' was the word that came out after she said his name." (Luke's family members are religious Catholics, and Luke is a former priest). "Someone I knew had the same type of lung tumor," I told Luke. "He passed away after having a lung collapse. Love him while he's here."

Luke said, "I will. We know his time is short."

"It's difficult for someone older to fight. Chemo and radiation are tiring and don't always extend life that long. Sometimes a person has lived their life and feels resigned to whatever their fate is. Allow him to do what he wants to do," I said. "Your family is close. Peace be with you and your family. I'll pray for all of you. Please remember our parents are supposed to go before we do."

Luke agreed. "You're a kind and wise woman. I love you for it."

I said, "If only I had your intelligence and photographic memory. I'll always love you unconditionally." I apologized to Luke for sending the text I'd sent in late winter. "I was angry," I said. "Time lessened it. It left many months ago, and I released it."

"I'm sorry I hurt you," Luke said. "I hoped you'd forgive me."

"I already have," I said. "Forgiveness is necessary."

A few weeks later, curious about how Luke's father's health was, I checked in. "How's your dad?"

"We set up hospice care for him," Luke said.

I could feel the heaviness in knowing this.

"He's still mobile, but he's regressing. According to the hospice nurse, he's going through the regular progression of the disease. Our family and Dad are all at peace with the inevitable outcome."

"I'm sorry you're going through it. As a family, you have strength and love."

Luke told me his family was caring for their patriarch.

"Know I pray for you and your family each morning while walking."

Luke thanked me and said, "You're a sweet woman."

Within a month, my intuition twigged me, and I looked up Luke's father's name online. Gulp... *His dad's obituary.* Seeing it made me want to reach out, but I hesitated because the obituary revealed Luke was now married. I smiled—I realized he'd been ready to marry for some time, and I was glad he'd found happiness. Knowing this allowed me to reflect upon my growth, and it was a wonderful feeling.

That same week I'd texted with Luke, I saw Larry at a family function. Our eyes locked, and that prompted me to check in with him by text. "I wanted to talk with you, but people were always around. I still think about and miss you. I haven't been out with anyone else. If you want it to stay in the past, tell me. I can remain just friends, too. If you want the same, let's talk."

After a few hours of me seeing he'd read my text, Larry responded, "I'd rather keep it in the past. You need someone that you can get serious with. And I'm not there. So, no hard feelings, please. You deserve somebody special."

No, I didn't want to become serious with anyone. I only wanted to spend more time with him. *I dislike it when men make assumptions about me.* But the time had come to move farther away from Larry. That was hard, and it was several months before I could attend family functions again. With his traumatic upbringing, he might never trust another woman or let them in. I hope he does.

Larry knew how spiritual I was, but he'd had a hard time understanding it. Sometimes I wish I could go back to when we first met. If my life hadn't been chaotic during round one, we might have stood the test of time. While I didn't let Erick go fully while I was with Larry, our relationship allowed me to let go of another layer of attachment so I could live in the moment with Larry.

Even with Larry's superficial and selfish personality, his hangups, and the pain he caused, I have no regrets about the time I spent with him. He was a blessing and later, he was a lesson for me. He was patient and accepted me, even when I was in my masculine energy and came on strong. I was told Divine had brought Larry into my life for me to have some fun… and we did. He treated me well overall, and I'll think of him fondly.

So, after hoping Larry would return to me, I had his answer. Once again, I had to move forward. Lonely after a chat with Samantha, I signed up on the Facebook dating app.

Chapter Ten

Matching on a Dating App

The evening I signed up on Facebook's dating app, I received a like from Kevin, a landscaping business owner. Kevin is four years younger than me and has a dark complexion and an oval face. He's thin, not much taller than me, with smiling brown eyes, salt-and-pepper hair, and a neatly trimmed goatee. *Handsome.* He looked relaxed and pleasant in his photos, but it was his profile that attracted me. He has a degree in journalism, is an avid sports fan, and loves dogs, hiking, and landscape photography.

Kevin's profile said, "I'm a hard-working guy who loves nothing more than being with my two boys. I enjoy the outdoors and cozy nights by the campfire. Fall is my favorite time of year." When I read he wasn't into "hookups" or one-night stands and wouldn't have sex on the first date, that was appealing. Kevin said he was looking for something real and someone to enjoy life with. Learning that he lived thirty minutes away and grew up in the same county as me sparked my interest. Also, his punctuation was impeccable, which impressed me!

Taking the plunge, I sent Kevin a like back, and the app matched us. He couldn't believe I knew his hometown. I told him my cousins (Sadie and her family) live there. It turned out Kevin played on a baseball team with a cousin of mine.

Through the app, Kevin told me he's been married and divorced twice, like me. He told me that he'd had an affair in his first marriage to Tara, and things were never the same between them. They eventually divorced. Jane, his second wife, now also his ex, is younger than him. In their marriage, she'd had an affair. They'd been good teammates for the kids, but the "it" factor was never there. Tara had addiction issues for years and died in a wreck while he was married to Jane.

Tara's death saddened me, especially for their son, Jeremy, twenty-one. His younger son, David, eleven, is from his second marriage. Jeremy has a terminal lung disease, but newer medications should extend his life for many years. David has a serious digestive condition that's manageable. Kevin sounded like a wonderful father who always puts his kids first. I admired that.

Kevin started a landscaping business during his first marriage, and he's had it for thirty-two years. He provides landscape design, mowing and maintenance, aeration, pruning, and tree removal. Twelve men work with him during the busy season. He's survived on little sleep, like me. Kevin told me that when he was in his twenties, he'd had long hair and had followed the Grateful Dead around for a year.

As we texted on the app, Kevin asked me, "What's your 'love language'?" His included quality time, words of affirmation, acts of service, physical touch, and gifts. The only difference in mine, I told him, was that for me, touch comes before acts of service, but they're equal in percentage.

Kevin told me he enjoys the single life but thinks life is more fun when you have someone to share it with. He hasn't found the person who clicks with him, but he said, "I hope to find someone to enjoy the little things in life with. Sometimes life is lonely, and it would be awesome to find my 'soulmate.' But I'm not holding my breath on that."

"Why did you get a divorce?" Kevin asked.

I explained that Greg and I had a good marriage for several years. However, things changed. I became resentful of Greg becoming a house husband, and I lost respect for him. Greg watched political shows and drank coffee, while I provided for our family—and grew unhappy.

I told Kevin about my fall and my spiritual awakening. Later, I'd connected with someone who was more than just a soulmate to me. I'd felt we'd incarnated in multiple lives. I'd never cheated in over twenty-four and a half years of marriage, but I'd never had a magnetic connection like that. I had an affair and filed for divorce two months later. It was settled right after our twenty-fifth wedding anniversary. "My ex is a good person and has since remarried," I told him. Kevin said he could see I wouldn't be interested in raising another child (which is what you're doing when your partner isn't doing their part). He said having a faithful partner is now huge for him.

He asked about my "fall." "Was it physical or metaphorical?" he asked.

I explained I'd fallen out of the shower and that the blow to my face had led to my spiritual awakening.

"If the man you were with was more than a soulmate, why aren't you still together?"

Oh boy… how to explain?

I wondered how Kevin, a potential love interest, would process all this information. I didn't reveal it all at once, but I knew I couldn't hide it, because if I want to have a chance at genuine happiness with anyone, I must reveal who I truly am and what happened.

It turned out Jane had had an affair with someone from their church before their physical separation, which had had many effects on Kevin's life. They'd stopped going to church once he found out.

Since I'd been honest with the hard truth, Kevin wanted to do the same. He doesn't judge people—as he said, it isn't his place to do that. I loved when he said he believes in destiny and fate but also that trials and tribulations strengthen us. Kevin revealed he's a functional alcoholic but has been sober for over two years. He blames himself for pushing Jane away and said that he used to drink to deal with his problems. He'd had his own awakening when he hit rock bottom and now lives a happy life free of alcohol and most of his troublesome thoughts. His relationship with his children is stronger, his business is flourishing, and his mind is clear. He said he's grateful for the blessings God has given him.

Kevin is a Libra, on the cusp of Scorpio, but told me he identifies as a Libra. Because I love astrology and the connection between signs, I knew we were compatible and that there was potential for something special to grow between us. We love the same musical genres, but he has an interest in country music I don't have. Also, we both love Harry Potter. He's identified as a Gryffindor and I as a Ravenclaw. We were born in the same hospital, and we had the same school teacher. We're both picky eaters, and scrambled eggs are our favorite. He loves older family photos, like me. He's also a workaholic. It's not uncommon for him to work fourteen-hour days, which I understand all too well.

Kevin asked if I'd be interested in a game he'd played once before. It's called "twenty questions." We'd take turns, and nothing would be off the table unless something made the other person uncomfortable.

"You can ask anything," he said. "Your answer has to be honest, and you can't ask a question that either of us has already asked. It's a great way to get to know someone."

During the twenty questions game, we talked about Kevin's alcoholism, my numbing out and struggles, and our pasts. It turns out rum is his drink of choice (so is mine), and we both smoke pot to help us sleep. When he asked what qualities I seek in a man, I listed compassion, humor, a non-judgmental nature, kindness, passion, honesty, emotional availability, a loving nature, living in the moment, authenticity, and trust.

He asked, "All in one guy?"

"Yes."

"How many guys are you talking to right now?"

"Just you."

Kevin told me he has had true love with only two women in his life. I learned more about Kevin's upbringing. His parents had separated when he was two, and he became "the man of the house" at a young age. He'd worked on a farm at age six and got his first job at thirteen. He'd shouldered the weight of adult responsibilities from a young age, juggling a full-time job while attending high school and college. His mom, Wendy, worked twelve-hour days, then she came home and slept. So, he'd learned early on to fend for himself. He said, "My mom is headstrong and sometimes we butt heads, but I know she's the right mother for me and I love her. She suffers from rheumatoid arthritis pain."

Kevin told me his dad was always a part of his life, but while he picked Kevin up on the weekends, he spent little time with him. Instead, his dad gave him a bunch of money and dropped him off at the arcade or bowling alley. It saddened me when he referred to it as a "Cat's in the Cradle" relationship—one in which one person just can't make time for another. This remained the case until Kevin became an adult. They grew closer after Kevin's first son was born. Still, while Kevin's dad wanted to spend more time with him as an adult, Kevin's life was busier with work, and he had his own family. However, they got closer in the years before his father's death.

Chapter Eleven

Meditating and Letting Go

It was time for my springtime Elohee retreat. While there, we attendees work on ourselves with sound healing, meditation, and other modalities. Relaxed and contemplative while a Reiki practitioner was working on me, I went into a meditative state. I saw a bright white light in the background and saw Jesus' crown of thorns. It took everything in me to remain in that moment when something I never expected to see came through my third eye: My Lord and Savior was there with me. I knew I was a redeemed and forgiven soul. *How does this happen? I'm not worthy.*

As the Reiki session ended, the practitioner asked me to visualize a golden ray of light. "The spirit guides interrupted me," she told me. "Spirit asked me to call in the violet flame."

The violet flame meditation helps in transmuting karma so one can neutralize suffering from negative cycles. It offers emotional healing, spiritual growth, a shift in karma, and has a high vibrational energy. One can transmute negativity into positivity.

We both called in the violet flame, and after we'd finished the Reiki session, I became emotional. I told the practitioner what I'd seen.

"Jesus has only come through in one other session I've done," she told me.

When I told her that the Violet Flame was affiliated with Twin Flames, she smiled and said, "Of course it is." (A year later, one of the spiritual cards I received randomly from the retreat leader at Elohee was the Violet Flame card!)

Later, when I lay in a hammock by the Elohee waterfall in a meditative state, I had a vision. I saw Jesus' crown of thorns behind me. In front of me, I saw God's energy—the same energy I'd seen at an Ayahuasca ceremony. I saw Erick's higher self. We were facing each other, holding hands between God's energy and Jesus' crown of thorns. That vision is etched into my memory.

With all the bad things I've done and actions I've taken, I'm still overwhelmed by the love I receive from the Higher Power. I'm trying everything to understand my higher calling. I know the lessons I've signed up for are difficult. I'm a broken soul and I'm working on reclaiming my power. I realize now I've always had my inner strength. However, I've given away my power and energy to people and situations I shouldn't have. It isn't selfish to put yourself first.

Brother

With the sadness I had experienced living in my home and the decrease in my earnings, I decided to move. Around the time I downsized my business, I started looking to purchase property near Sadie. Homes have skyrocketed in price since I purchased my home, so I researched property values in my townhouse complex online. I discovered that six months ago, Jeff, Erick's brother, had purchased a home on the same street I live on.

In a town of over 60,000, how could this happen? Was it him? Yes. He lives 200 feet from my front door. I felt vulnerable and no longer invisible. I didn't like it. *Why didn't my intuition alert me? Does he know who I am?*

From then on, when I took Crystal on walks to the dog park twice a day, I was observant. One early summer morning, I was walking by his house and saw Jeff outside. I couldn't look him in the eye but could see how much the brothers looked alike. He's handsome, younger than Erick, but not as tall, with a smaller frame.

Something feels like Jeff knows who I am.

Going to my mailbox or walking Crystal, I was anxious, fearing I'd see Jeff. Jeff's habits were like mine—he was home often with little company. One morning, I was pulling out of my garage and saw Erick's vehicle in his driveway. My heart palpitated. When I returned home, I reviewed my security footage, which showed he was only at Jeff's for a brief time.

I saw Erick's vehicle at Jeff's three times. I prayed Karen wouldn't find me again or go with Erick to Jeff's. Luckily, that never happened (that I'm aware of). With Roman living with me, I felt safer than I would've had I been alone.

⚓

Roman, my twenty-two-year-old son, met a woman, Beth, through mutual gaming friends. She came to visit us and stayed for a few days. One day, I noticed a "Plan B" emergency contraceptive wrapper in the garbage. My heart sank. A wave of sadness washed over me. This was happening way too fast. I shared my concerns with them—and gave them a reality check. It fell on deaf ears. I said, "Whatever you do, don't get pregnant."

I hadn't realized that they were planning for her to stay for an extended period, and I told Roman, "You have to move out. You aren't going to play house under my roof."

Within two weeks, three things happened rapid-fire. Roman told me he was moving up North with Beth, eight hours away, and five days later, they moved. A week later, I asked my business coach, Mark, "Is it time to withdraw from the pain office I work with?" His answer was, "Yes." A week after that, Brian said he wanted peace between us.

I texted Brian, "There's peace, but I can't be in your life." He's lived a hard life and had been living in a motel for a while. His health wasn't good, and he was afraid of dying. I didn't want his life to end harshly, but felt that the way he's lived, he'd die before his natural time.

As a mother, it was hard watching Roman move hundreds of miles away. *It's a different kind of heartbreak.* Two months later, I received a call.

"Are you sitting?" Roman asked.

"Yes."

"I'm going to be a father."

I was surprised. He'd only met her five months ago!

I'm going to be a grandmother at fifty-four.

A month later, Roman called again. Again, he asked, "Are you sitting down?"

Oh boy.

"It's twins!"

Twins run on both sides of the family (at least eight sets on Granny's side), and Grandpa was an identical twin. Twins run in Beth's family, too. A month later, I found out it was a boy and a girl.

Although Roman and Beth didn't choose a traditional route, my cup of love runs over for them. I think accepting this situation has been one of my toughest lessons as a parent. I must let my son live his own life as a father. I'm alone now, but I'm not a helicopter parent—it's time for Roman to learn his own lessons. Despite my imperfections, I hope he remembers me as a loving mother who raised and taught him well, and that he instills love, kindness, and patience in his children.

Roman leaving home left me with empty nest syndrome, and I had all the "firsts"—all those first holidays alone. Knowing I was alone for Mother's Day for the first time, Kevin was attentive. We'd been communicating, and he told me that for a year, he'd been involved with a lady he'd known in his youth, Cory. She was a year younger than him. *His first kiss.* She was separated from her husband. They'd broken up around the same time Larry and I did.

Kevin wanted to resume our "twenty questions" game. By now, we'd already surpassed twenty questions, and I didn't see it slowing soon. We talked about vulnerability, and he said he wished he could be vulnerable. Kevin thought he could be with the right person, but said he fears being hurt.

To help Kevin understand me and the depth of heartbreak I've experienced, I shared *My Twin Flame Journey* with him.

Kevin started reading the book. He asked, "What's the relationship between you and Erick?"

"It ended four years ago," I said.

"How old is he?"

"Eight years older than me."

A few days later, after reading three chapters, Kevin asked, "Why did you want me to read the book?" Kevin is a loyal man, and his wife had an affair. "Those two factors made it hard for me not to read your book from Greg's point of view," he said. He asked about my spiritual beliefs.

"I didn't want you to find out later what had transpired and think I'd lied." *I won't mislead anyone.* "The events that turned my life upside down are important for someone who is considering being with me to know." I hadn't divulged my Twin Flame connection to Chris, with whom I'd had a relationship after Erick. Chris was a spiritual person and had visions of seeing Erick and me together. He said, "You don't belong to me," and broke up with me. It took a while for me to heal from that relationship. *I won't repeat what happened with Chris.*

When we were discussing our ex-spouses, I told Kevin that whenever Greg raised his voice to me, I closed myself off. *That's because of Daddy's explosive temper.*

Kevin said that he and Jane never argued—she just wouldn't communicate. On the infrequent occasion he raised his voice, she'd shut down and played the victim. That left him feeling like a mean person, when all he was doing was trying to get his point across. When she needed to convey something important, she avoided discussing it—she emailed him from the bedroom while he sat on the couch.

Having internalized my feelings for most of my life, I see how that can happen.

It turned out Kevin has been heartbroken twice and shell-shocked once. "I don't know if I was heartbroken with the third one. Just surprised."

Kevin asked, "How many men have caused you genuine grief?"

"Five."

A month after finding me on social media, Kevin asked me on a date but had to cancel because of an unexpected issue with his youngest son. "Can we take a raincheck?" he asked.

"Yes. What traits are you looking for in a woman?"

"Personality, depth, intelligence, and a sense of humor," he said. "Looks aren't the first thing I look for in a woman, and I lean toward a thicker woman."

Knowing Kevin had seen my photos, I asked, "Do you consider me 'thicker'?"

"You're the size I find most attractive."

Chapter Twelve

Having a Perfect First Date

Conversations with Kevin seemed to be of a non-judgmental nature, and we agreed on most things. However, when I told him I read Tarot cards and used crystals, Kevin was taken aback. Still, I know couples where one is religious and the other spiritual, and their relationships work.

Kevin told me he's seeking answers where his faith is concerned. He's a cradle Catholic but fell away from the faith some time ago. Since he quit drinking, he's become much closer to God. But he told me he has many questions. He's searching for spiritual answers, including wanting to know what the afterlife holds. Kevin thinks God put me in his life for a reason—maybe for multiple reasons. He's been asking questions about my awakening because, he said, he felt he was on the verge of something similar. He couldn't explain it but said it's a combination of a feeling he has plus the dreams he's having. Kevin is a realist and, until now, has been interested only in what's tangible. He used to have a closed mind, he said, but he's grown and has become more open.

Kevin surprised me a few days later when he said, "I want to be in love again. I haven't felt that in a long time."

"After Erick, I didn't think I could ever love again," I said. "The hurt I experienced can still make me cry. It took time, but I've loved since then. There are strong possibilities for us… if we ever meet." *Even with hurt, I think my heart loves more than most people's hearts do.*

"I don't fall in love easily," Kevin said. "I live a busy life. It doesn't leave enough time. I need to prioritize better."

"Do you want to prioritize time with me?"

"I do," he said. "I'm not used to prioritizing things I want. I haven't been on a date for several months. Any free time I have, I give to my kids."

"I respect and understand that," I said.

"The last woman I dated got jealous of my children. I think I caused that. It opened my eyes. I didn't prioritize myself or her. I always put my boys before her. I needed to make up for lost time with my kids, because even though I was there for them, I wasn't entirely 'there' when I drank."

"Do you see yourself being emotionally and physically available? I thought we hadn't met because you work so much, but your words help me understand. Although I'd be disappointed, I'd understand if you need to focus on your kids and don't have time for me. Just say so. It'd be easier to know now than later."

"You keep saying 'just say' as if you want me to say I don't have time for you. That's not the case. We need to plan a date."

This conversation triggered me. "When we started texting, I thought you were looking for something similar to what I was looking for. Your profile showed that. I saw how busy you are with work and your kids. I had patience, which hasn't always been a virtue of mine. When I first asked why it ended between you and Cory, you said it was because she lived in another state, and neither of you would move. When you said you never made time for her, that was my trigger. I told you that's why I stopped seeing Larry, because he wouldn't make time for me. I questioned why you activated the dating app if you didn't intend to follow through with meeting me. I've wanted to meet you. It's been three months." I felt anxiety creep up.

"I don't like it when you ask me the same questions over and over," he said.

"I'm not asking the same thing repeatedly. You hadn't shared about not making time for her before. When I say 'just say,' it's because that's how I try to make it easier for someone to tell me they don't want to pursue things. Do you see yourself being available to me?"

"It has to start with a date. Would you be interested in having dinner at an Italian restaurant? Then we can go to a park in the state capital."

"That sounds wonderful," I said. "I love Italian food."

Super excited, I purchased a pair of black scalloped shorts, a periwinkle summer sweater top, black sandals, and had a fresh pedicure and facial. There was a chance of rain that evening, so I'd have frizzy hair, but I didn't care. We met at the restaurant.

Kevin was handsome but smaller than most men I'm attracted to. But I liked what I saw. He wore a grey tee shirt, shorts, sneakers, and carried a tall tumbler of coffee. I couldn't resist giving him a hug. He was warm and friendly, as I thought he would be. His dark eye color could be called Johnny-Depp or M&M-candy brown. We walked up the steps to our table. Our conversation and laughter were good, and things felt natural between us. Kevin was curious about my use of Ayahuasca, as he's used mushrooms in the past. Our meal was delicious. He's a good tipper, too.

After our meal, Kevin asked me to follow him in my car to a well-known park. We both parked close to a building with large pillars that had gods and goddesses on them. We walked and talked, and he took my hand. It felt good. It's what I'd wanted: romance. His weathered, hard-working dark hand contrasted against my fair skin. I loved that he had Irish and Cherokee Native American ancestors—that's what's in my DNA, too.

I'd brought an umbrella, and we sat on a swing under an enormous tree. It sheltered us for a while, but a few raindrops landed on my head and arms. It was romantic being with him in the rain. We talked and connected more until the temperature dropped, and then we walked, holding hands, until we reached my vehicle. He sat in my car with me a little longer.

Kevin wanted to see the music I had on my phone and saw my varied musical taste. As our date was ending, I let him take the lead. He reached out to hug me. As he released me, he stopped close to my face, as if seeing if I agreed to a kiss. It was respectful—a *good first kiss*. "Let me know when you get home," he said. We said goodbye and went our separate ways.

On my way home, I knew Kevin was special and was going to be an important part of my life. Erick wasn't on my mind at all during my date, a first since our separation. After I returned home, Kevin texted. "Thanks for a nice time. The rain made it more enjoyable," he said.

"I enjoyed it, too. I appreciated the great dinner and the conversation. Thanks for a perfect first date."

Chapter Thirteen

Achieving Higher Consciousness During Ayahuasca Journeys

After returning from my recent Ayahuasca journey and receiving the message that I was a healer, I found stones that would allow me to help others. I asked for guidance from mediums and healers. One healer told me about Archangel Raphael, who's in charge of physical healing. She told me to imagine a green ball of healing energy when trying to help others. Green is associated with the heart chakra, which symbolizes healing, unconditional love, and empathy. When I visualize this energy, the ball is fluorescent green with white energy sparks arcing from it.

My favorite crystals, which are for the third eye, throat, and heart chakras, sit on my dining room table. While holding the crystals, I concentrate on and visualize bright green healing energy. I knew who I wanted to help first. In recent months, my business consultant, Mark, had mentioned that his wife, Lori, had received a diagnosis of rheumatoid arthritis. After my world imploded after Erick, when I was uncertain of the outcome of my business, Mark had helped me in countless ways. I prayed about it and asked spiritually if it was okay to do this, and received a "Yes." Because I had no formal training, I did what I felt I should do intuitively. People pray for others all the time, ask for their healing, so this is my spiritual equivalent. I wanted to help Lori, if that's what God intended. Lori became part of my morning prayers. I prayed for her relief from symptoms affiliated with the disease and for her to be supported.

While pushing healing energy out, I prayed, asking Archangel Raphael to work with me to send healing energy to Lori. After each morning walk, I came home and worked with the crystals while praying for her. This went on for several months. I researched the crystals to help her and took two stones—a small heart-shaped rose quartz and carnelian—to my next appointment with Mark. "How's Lori?" I asked.

"In recent months, she hasn't experienced any flare-ups," he said.

"I've got two crystals for her," I said. "If she's open to it, will you give them to her?"

"She's willing to try anything," he said.

I can't be certain that what I did helped Lori, but I'd like to think so.

I reached out to a respected spiritual friend and mentor, who believes I'm becoming a conduit, a channel, for distance healing. In recent months, because of changes in my vibrational energy and trying to heal myself from setbacks, I've delayed focusing on my development as a healer, but in the coming months, I'll regroup and fulfill that part of my soul contract. It's a calling I can't ignore because my heart loves others deeply. As an empath, knowing someone is in pain hurts me. With God's love and support, I will continue to develop as a healer. I'm grateful for Ayahuasca, which has allowed me to see this part of my purpose.

Ayahuasca

Over nine Ayahuasca journeys in two years, I experienced the healing power of plant medicine. Each journey is different, but there are common themes. I wish I could show others the color and intensity of what I see as our New Earth, where heaven and Earth become one. But I can't explain or draw the images I've seen. Most of the colors are sharp blues, purples, and greens on a background of brilliant, blinding white.

The shades of spiritual color I see are difficult to take in through my spiritual eye (better known as "the third eye"), the connection between the physical and spiritual worlds. It's in the center of the forehead between the eyebrows and provides perception beyond ordinary sight. It's associated with intuition and linked to the pineal gland within the brain. One counselor at Ayahuasca asked me if I see fractal images. That doesn't even come close to what appears in my visions. The detailed intricacy I experience—though spiritual during an Ayahuasca journey—can best be compared to the so-called Pink Mosque, Nasir al-Molk in Shiraz, Iran, when the sunlight streams through the stained-glass windows. The "Ayahuascan colors" are brilliant, and the intricate design and dazzling beauty of the mosque is the closest earthly likeness to what I see in my Ayahuasca visions. It's difficult to maintain a memory of that otherworldly splendor when one returns to the mundane reality of our everyday world.

When ingesting Ayahuascan medicine, there's always the possibility of vomiting. It's better known as "the purge." I've tried to not vomit, as I didn't see it as necessary, but I've now learned that was ego-based thinking. I metabolize Ayahuasca quickly, likely because I've journeyed more and carry less fear as I increase the dosage. The most I've ever taken at one time is one and three quarters of a tablespoon—and even then, a small part of the dose remains on the sides of the cup. It's difficult to swallow it—it tastes disgusting. The facilitators gave me mapacho (also called Aztec tobacco) to smoke and a small lemon wedge to taste before and after I chugged the nastiness. Before journeys, I ask God, "Let me live through your love, light, grace, and Jesus' compassion."

Once Ayahuasca activates, beyond-bright colors become part of me. The white is so dazzling, and the images are sharper than anything I've ever seen. I want to remember all I can. Unlike other participants I talk to, who experience basic visions or see loved ones who have passed, I can talk to God. Yes, I know how that sounds, but it's true—on half of my journeys, I've seen God's energy. It's like the sun, but bigger and more brilliant, with unending shades of orange with browns on its surface.

During my first daytime journey, I brought several belongings with me, including my cell phone, which was in my bag. I didn't realize you weren't supposed to bring your cell phone when taking part in Ayahuasca. My phone was on silent, and near the end of my journey, I had a sudden urge to text Luke, the ex-priest (something I've since learned you shouldn't do in a sacred ceremony). But the words I had typed wouldn't send... it was as if I'd kept backspacing and erasing, but I hadn't. After trying a second time, I saw the letters in each word backspace and delete, leaving my screen blank: all without my fingers touching the keyboard! It was surreal. Whatever my thoughts had been, Divine didn't want me to send the message.

In one Ayahuasca session, I was aware enough to look down. I was standing in a faceless crowd in a large stadium. I looked down at my body. I knew I was older and was wearing a white priestess robe, and my long grey hair flowed down my shoulders. My hands, palms, and fingers were spread open, and energy was shooting out from my fingertips. I was healing others. Intuitively, I remembered, "I'm a healer who will help heal others in the future." Overwhelmed, I sat up on my mat and whispered, "I don't know how to do this."

I learned about Ayahuasca from Erick. He'd wanted to take an Ayahuasca journey with his son, but because he's an alcoholic and takes medication that could interact with Ayahuasca and cause him harm, on my last night journey, I made a special request: I asked God to allow Erick to see what I saw. Sharing my visions with him may be the only way he can see the Ayahuasca experience. I thought he'd be at home late on a Saturday night, and he'd likely be watching television. So I felt it would be an ideal time to invite his soul along on this magical journey, even if only ethereally. During that journey, there was a terrible summer thunderstorm with lightning, which seemed to elevate my awareness.

In my Ayahuasca journeys, as a Twin Flame, I seek to connect with both twins' higher selves. Before my mommy make-over surgery, I used to feel Erick's energy in my lower middle abdomen, under my navel. (The sensation was like riding in a car and going over a small hill.) But since the surgery, when the nerves in my lower abdomen were cut, I'm numb in that area. I no longer feel Erick physically, as I once did. Intuitively, though, when he's thinking about me, I know.

Releasing and Forgiving Daddy

My Ayahuasca journeys brought up memories of unhealed wounds I've suppressed. Not just about Erick, but also about Daddy. Most of my close childhood friends weren't aware of my Daddy's actions until they read my first book. During one journey, when I understood Daddy has been in a life review since his death, surprisingly, I didn't feel sympathy for him. As I shared earlier, his physical, verbal, and emotional abuse toward Mama was horrific. He beat Brian severely. If Divine still had Daddy in life review, there had to be a reason. I thought: *Let him stay and rewatch... over and over.* That was wrong of me. I realized it was time to let go of what he'd done to Mama and Brian and my guilt over having seen and heard the abuse. I'd forgiven him, but I hadn't released the related pain. That's a necessary part of the healing process, and we can't skip it. Often, over the years, I've sat in my chair in the evenings, replaying situations about Daddy. As I noted earlier, my relationship with him continued to trigger my PTSD.

However, on that last journey, it was about my healing of Daddy's wounding, when I asked that he be released from his ongoing life review. As I mentioned earlier, two mediums have told me Daddy was desperate for me to forgive him.

I already have.

I asked God to release Daddy from his life review. Two years was long enough. Was that for me to decide? No, it wasn't, but I believe now that it's because of my pain that he's remained there. I'm not vindictive, so I dug deep. I wanted it to be over. No more suffering. After I made that intention, my first real purge happened. This time, I allowed it to come. That night, I was unsteady. I left my mat with help from a volunteer. On each journey, volunteers ensure participants make it safely outside the sacred lodge. Outside, volunteers oversee us, too. There were seventy participants. I sat by the warm fire reflecting on my journey and was "the last one standing" that night. It was after 2:00 a.m., and I was escorted back to my room to sleep. It's been two years since that journey—two years of reflection. I no longer dwell on Daddy's abuse. It will always be a part of my memories, but it no longer defines me or causes pain. I released the pain he caused. I don't know why I chose him to be my father for this lifetime, as part of my soul contract, and why I had to learn the affiliated lessons with him, but the abuse I witnessed and heard that's been my constant companion since childhood no longer torments me. I acknowledge that part of my life, and with gratitude, I walk forward and don't look back.

Reminiscing, Daddy loved me in his own way, but never the way I wanted or needed to be loved. How it was that I only witnessed and heard his physical abuse of Mama and Brian, and was never hurt physically, is something I no longer question. It's most likely because I was a girl. Yes, the memories will always be there, but they are fading. We're in control of what we hold on to, but release and surrender of traumatic situations is the goal. I realized this release was the purpose of me attending Ayahuasca. It wasn't about me connecting to Erick's higher self. Ayahuasca gave me what I *needed*, not what I wanted.

As the Ayahuasca experience ends, it's hard to let the visions fade from memory. It's like waking up from a dream with only fragments of it clinging to your awareness—and then they're gone. They're hard to hold on to! But the most important parts remain. It's important to take time to record your thoughts and the insights and wisdom you return with. Sadly, I'm lazy doing that part. I sometimes send myself text messages to keep those thoughts available, and I jot down a few words to help trigger my thoughts at a later time. I wish I'd written more about my individual journeys.

Channeled words that have come through during Ayahuasca's journeys include, "You're special," "You're ready," "You're pure," "You're love," "Be still," "Be the change," and "You're a Divine being." During my Ayahuasca journey, when I asked for Daddy to be released from life review, I channeled the words, "There's nobody like my little girl." I'm embracing those special messages.

During reintegration, Ayahuasca counselors work with you, and you share your Ayahuasca experience in a small group gathering. While talking about seeing myself healing others, and hearing that I was a Divine being, I became emotional. However, if the Divine is tasking me to help others, I'll do whatever I can to integrate my Divine purpose and complete my soul contract. I'm goal-oriented—I don't want to disappoint God! In my small group, after hearing about my journey, a young woman called me a "High Priestess." I smiled. In the Tarot, the High Priestess is a powerful symbol of spiritual knowledge and intuition. I've known that I'm a High Priestess for a while but never said it out loud. I'm glad someone saw and recognized the real me.

Last Daytime Journey

One hot morning in Orlando, Florida, a group I was with was part of my last outdoor daytime Ayahuasca journey. I couldn't flow into it. There was construction next door, and I was sitting between a man of Jewish faith, who was speaking or praying in words I didn't comprehend, and a young lady was giggling. Between them and the construction noise, I couldn't block it all out. I raised my hand and asked the facilitator if I could go inside the lodge. I lay down on my individual black mat inside with some other journeyers.

While attending spiritual events where I'm seated or laying down, I cover up with my vintage Divine Feminine sarong blanket against my skin. It's a thin, goldenrod summer quilt made of two vintage sarongs, with a design depicting several Hindu women on it. It has crimson red and aquamarine blue accents. I bought it at the Elohee gift shop during one of my earlier retreats. When I drink Aya, my body temperature increases, but if I become cold, I put additional blankets on top of my Elohee blanket. Someone looking at me while in my full spiritual presence might refer to me as a priestess, minus the flowing skirt.

To prepare for each journey, I take at least twenty-five crystals to hold and squeeze during the ceremony—stones related to love, healing, the heart, the throat, and the third-eye chakras. Each has a purpose (I recommend going to a reputable crystal store and also researching stones online to find out which crystals might work best for you). Some of my most spiritual stones include: a triangular-square Shiva Lingam in feminine tones of brown and beige; a black, egg-shaped masculine Shiva Lingam; a purplish Nirvana quartz; pale yellow Libyan desert glass; a blue angelite encased in a silver basket; a clear Lemurian quartz; a black prophecy stone; a pale yellow golden healer quartz; a greenish-blue dumortierite; and a green seraphinite with white angel wings. I wear two powerful necklaces of grey guardianite and purple sugilite and three stone mala necklaces. A mala is the spiritual equivalent of a Catholic rosary. One mala is made of yellow calcite, green aventurine, and orangey-red fire agate, for feminine energy. My pretty purple agate is for insight, strength, and clarity. But my favorite mala is for one seeking tranquility by balancing yin and yang energies—it offers balance and stability. It includes multi-colored impression jasper and agate, brown wenge wood, and bright aqua cords. I complete my spiritual wardrobe with two rings (protective mystic topaz and communicative larimar) and at least ten crystal bracelets. I've never seen anyone during any of my journeys with as many stones as I bring.

I squeezed those stones in my hands during my journey and found comfort and strength in them when things got deep. One of my favorite stones is my blue angelite that's encased in a silver basket. It escaped my hand and rolled toward another participant. A volunteer retrieved it. I saw gnats around me inside the lodge. I was trying to shoo them, but then I regained my wits and raised my hand. A volunteer came over.

"I know they aren't real," I said, "but are there gnats in here?"
She smiled, and said, "No."

Gnats can have a positive spiritual meaning, including change, transformation, resilience, and persistence.

While at Ayahuasca, anything can happen. Once I saw musical notes in my third eye. Once, during meditation, the Salem witch trials dropped inside my head. My last journey was just what I needed, and after our group integration, which combined our unique perspectives and experiences, it was time to fly home.

When I share my journeys with my best friend, Samantha, she expresses her doubt and worry about me "going to extreme measures" for my beliefs. She struggles with me being drawn to spirituality because she's become religious since COVID-19 (but doesn't attend church). We're opposites in our beliefs about spiritual subjects. She worries about my soul after I die. My thirst to learn more and become who I'm supposed to be during this lifetime makes her uncomfortable. She doesn't understand my desire to go to Ayahuasca to heal.

"You don't have to worry about me," I said. "You need to worry about yourself. If our friendship is going to remain intact, we have to agree to disagree."

After returning from the last Ayahuasca journey two years ago, I haven't felt the calling to return. Plant medicine isn't for everyone, but if you go to Ayahuasca's mat, you can open your heart and heal. Visions and messages allow for expansion of the mind.

Seeking Spiritual Guidance

After my return from my Ayahuasca journey, I told Kevin, "A lot was going on spiritually, beyond my level of comprehension. I'm contacting Luke for guidance. He's married now, so our meeting will only be for him to help me interpret what I've seen. Meeting him is platonic and for spiritual guidance on the next leg of my journey."

"Thanks for letting me know," Kevin said.

I texted Luke: "I'm sorry about your dad." I had prayed for his family's healing, so I asked, "How are you and your family? I saw your dad's obituary the weekend after he passed away."

"It's been a hard few months," Luke replied. "Easter and Father's Day were hard this year. It's still a strange reality now that my parents are gone."

"First holidays are always the worst. No matter how old we are, we miss our parents." I asked, "Would you have time to discuss the things I saw at my retreat?"

"I would like us to meet and talk."

"Will your wife support us meeting?" I texted. *I have no romantic feelings toward Luke and wouldn't have wanted her to be concerned.* "Please tell her I'm involved with someone and wouldn't do anything to harm or jeopardize your marriage."

"I think she'll support us in the meeting."

"Congratulations on your marriage, Luke. I'm happy for you." Being unsure of what he might say about my visions,

I said, "I've been seeing images and symbols more when I close my eyes. I've seen myself in a white priestess robe with energy shooting out of my fingers. Although I know that huge milestones in my spiritual path will come into alignment, I'm unsure how I'll accomplish it but trust in Divine."

Luke texted, "I know you're already a source of healing and blessing to others."

I thanked him. "It goes beyond that. I channeled a message that I'm a divine being."

"What do you think all of it means?"

"In the future, I'll be tasked with doing things I don't know how to do. It scares me because I don't know how to do it. I'm a regular person who's made many mistakes. People might think I'm crazy if I say it. I've become stronger in my spirituality and am connected to God."

"Being connected to God is a wonderful place to be."

"You kept coming to me during my Ayahuasca journeys. I saw myself seemingly blessing people. I can only imagine how that sounds to you."

He asked, "What feelings did it bring up?"

"My honest response? I don't know how to do this. I'm being tasked with helping humanity."

Luke said, "I promise I'm not trying to be obvious. Have you asked God what this means?"

I replied, "No. I will, though. It's overwhelming.

Luke believes God doesn't leave us alone to figure out His plan, especially when He wants to bring health, hope, and healing to others. "Ask Him what it means and what He wants you to do. It will be revealed to you."

"Thank you. That helps me."

"I'm happy to help if I can."

"You just did."

"I believe God has huge plans for you."

"Do you think that's why you found me?" I asked. (Luke found me on social media.) "I think you may guide me through this, whatever it may be."

"If that's the reason, I'd be honored to help you."

"I think we came together because you had to activate something within me. Would you be willing to help me understand? I've seen coded images, like light codes, but I can't draw them. This is big and in the highest good."

Luke texted, "You're an extraordinary woman. I love you."

"Thank you, Luke. I love you, too." *We share a Divine love and connection.* "Please don't take this the wrong way, but I saw a medium. When she told me you and I are part of a spiritual monad, I assumed you would teach me. She asked me, 'You think he's the teacher?' It took me a minute to absorb that. Monads are complex, and it's difficult to grasp the concept. I don't have the religious or book knowledge you do, but I have spiritual knowledge."

Later, I texted Luke information about the higher self and spiritual monads and asked him to review it so he could explain it to me.

The day had come to meet with Luke. During lunch at the barbeque restaurant, Luke and I shared a friendly hug. I let go before he did. He looked happy and had lost weight. We had less than an hour to talk and catch up. The restaurant was busy, with the rich and savory scent of barbeque hanging in the air, making my mouth water.

I felt as close to him as I ever had. Our exchange was friendly and light. Curious, I asked, "When did you marry Bridget?"

He smiled at me across the small table. "We got married last October."

That was six months after I'd cut communication with him. They met through a dating app. He said they knew on their second date they would be together.

"I'm glad you found her," I said, taking a bite of my chicken barbeque. "I've prayed for you to find her."

Luke thanked me. "Your pathway in prayer is amazing. Is Kevin okay with our meeting?"

"He's aware and seemed okay with it. If he isn't, then he isn't the man for me."

I asked Luke if Bridget knew about what had transpired in our relationship. "I didn't divulge the intimacy of our relationship," he said with a familiar, knowing smile.

I'll always remember our Divine and intimate connection fondly.

His blue eyes took on a serious tone, and he looked deep into my eyes. "Can I share something with you?"

"Yes."

During our conversation, Luke made some comments that caught me off guard and helped me understand something important. I realized that he'd experienced the true essence of my Divine Feminine energy, and it had left a lasting impact. This taught me that masculine energies remain magnetized by an authentic connection to the Divine Feminine, even after relationships end.

He wanted to clarify whether I'd seen sacred geometry after we were intimate.

I reminded him of the Fibonacci spiral I'd seen.

Luke had none of the answers I'd hoped for. I'd believed that since he was once a priest, he'd be able to give me the spiritual guidance I needed. He didn't. I was disappointed.

He only said that I'm doing the right thing as long as I'm not in ego.

I'm not. *I want to remain friends with Luke and value his spiritual guidance, but I can never meet with him again in person, as I'm unsure of his intent toward me.*

Finding Healing Crystals

As I digested my meeting with Luke and his inappropriate statements, I drove to my favorite crystal store, looking for stones to use while healing others. While at the store, I read descriptions of what each stone does spiritually. I find I'm drawn to some crystals and pendulums intuitively. The pendulum is a divinity tool to help a user tap into the all-knowing and intuition within the self. The pendulum transmits energy between the unconscious and conscious mind and helps make sense of electromagnetic fields around us. You can hold the pendulum in different ways when asking questions. My preferred method is to hold it between my index finger and thumb. You connect with it and establish the way the pendulum will reply with "Yes" and "No" answers. The best way is to make a statement and see if the pendulum responds correctly. When I receive an answer for myself or others, I sometimes clarify it by using a second pendulum. It's amazing how accurate they are.

My favorite crystal store has a butterfly-shaped amethyst chair inside the store. When you walk inside, Eastern music with chanting is playing. I sat on the chair and felt peaceful. Mandi, the lovely medium and medical empath, was working that day, and I shared with her that in my Ayahuasca experience, I learned that I'm supposed to help heal others—although this isn't all I'll do. I was unsure of the best crystals to help me accomplish this part of my soul contract. "Can you help?"

She smiled and walked toward a large, irregular-shaped clear crystal quartz. Mandi told me it would help magnify and amplify my energy intention (it helps someone to project energy). I felt drawn to a large, hexagram-shaped troilite stone pillar. It was sky blue and steel grey and reminded me of Egyptian sand at night. It had a formation like two eyes looking outward.

She said, "Troilite is for intuition, meditation, and emotional healing."

I picked each crystal up. Each weighed five pounds and had a sharp point at the top. She agreed that these were my stones. They were quite expensive, but she gave me a discount.

When the purchase was complete, she told me I'd help many people with the crystals. I believe she discounted the stones because her guides gave her information I wasn't privy to. I was excited to work with the crystals and drove home. I wasn't sure how Kevin would feel about my meeting with Luke and the crystals I'd purchased, but I hoped he would accept everything that had unfolded.

⚓

After I told him I was meeting with Luke, Kevin's texts had decreased. My intuition was bothering me, and that made me anxious. When I texted to ask if everything was okay, he only said, "I'll talk to you later." Our texting resumed, and I tried not to worry.

We talked about vulnerability, and he said he's the polar opposite—his inability to be vulnerable is his biggest character flaw.

My intuition and anxiety were in hyper-drive. A week went by, and I texted Kevin again. "What do you want to talk about?"

He texted back: "I'm not sure that you and I can be more than friends. Since your 'Twin Flame' and the man who cost you your marriage and your son is still someone you need to have in your life… I'm not interested in falling into the same problems that Greg did. I think you're a good person, but I'm a one-woman guy. I'm not interested in sharing you with the love of your life. I understand, but I can't do it. These are the reasons I don't make myself vulnerable."

Big misunderstanding!

"Why do you think I still need to have him in my life? I haven't seen him in almost three years. Why are you thinking you're sharing me?"

He said, "You met with him the other day."

"Kevin, I didn't meet with him. I met with Luke, the former priest I'd been involved with. It was platonic, and for the next part of my spiritual journey. I want you, not him."

Kevin was confused. "Wait, what?! You said you were meeting with him."

"Luke is married, and his wife knew we were having lunch. It was about things I saw at Ayahuasca and the healing I'm supposed to do."

He asked, "This is NOT Luke from your book?!"

Again, I explained who Luke and Erick were.

Kevin acknowledged his total confusion.

"I wouldn't do that to you. I see genuine possibilities with you. That's something that doesn't happen every day for me."

"I'm sorry. I feel like an idiot. I only had a problem with it because I thought you were meeting with Erick."

"My meeting with Luke was only for an hour at a restaurant." My clairsentience felt heightened. My Tarot cards had revealed recently that there was a third party in my relationship with Kevin, which made me think there was someone else on his end. (That energy can be related to a situation with three people involved, the impact or influence of another person, or a love triangle.) Even though I read Tarot, sometimes reading my own situation is difficult. Many readers can either read their own situation or others', but not both.

Kevin said, "Jane asked me if casual sex was off the table for us. Any random man has what she's looking for. It's off the table for me."

That bothered me, so I shared a photo of the spread of his cards that showed betrayal and the third party with him.

⚓

Kevin replied, "Within two days of Jane's proposition, Cory reached out. She wanted to come to my home. I told her she couldn't."

Even though Kevin had turned her away too, it bothered me that two former partners had reached out to him. It activated my rejection wound.

I wanted to know more about Cory.

"Things between us are... complicated," Kevin said. "Cory was my first 'puppy love,' and we've maintained contact over the years. We dated a year ago, but the distance became too much to overcome. She's the closest thing to me having a Twin Flame. Things can't work for us for many reasons. Now, we're friends."

My intuition was causing me acute anxiety, so I asked more questions. Cory was married but separated at the time she and Kevin were seeing each other. Since then, she's reunited with her husband.

"I apologized to her husband for my role in making his life more difficult," Kevin said.

"Knowing of my affair, I didn't think you had judged me, but you had certain feelings about it. You had an affair with her. I know the situation isn't the same, but why did my affair elicit powerful emotion within you?"

"I think because she was going through a divorce, and it didn't last as long."

"You dated her for a year. I was involved with Erick for less than nine months."

"I thought your affair was longer."

Kevin knew the Ayahuasca journeys I was taking were releasing pain from parental wounds that had been exacerbated by my relationship with Erick. I haven't been able to move forward until now. Although I had elevated anxiety, I could see things were moving in the right direction.

The time had come for us to have our next date. We planned on dinner and going to see a Jennifer Lawrence movie. I liked how natural it was to hold his hand, and to have him rest it on my thigh. We laughed during the movie. Both of us felt the energy between us and knew it was a good thing. He could see a potential future between us.

He said, "You have incredibly kind eyes."

I replied, "Thank you."

I waited to tell Kevin about Luke's inappropriate comments until our date. All he could say was, "That's messed up."

Chapter Fourteen

Receiving Divine Protection

Eight months after being told I had no evidence of breast cancer in 2022, I completed my first breast cancer walk at a local mall. The sunny morning was cool, but it warmed up. There was music and dancing, and the local media covered the walk. Many teams raised money to finance breast cancer research. I wore the same costume I'd worn at the Mud Run. I walked the course with other participants—it took under forty-five minutes.

Near the end of the walk, people were cheering for the women crossing the finish line. I saw an older Caucasian man in a pink costume congratulating each of us by holding his hand out for each of us to tap and then presenting us with a medal. His name was Wayne, and he seemed nice. He appeared to be about twenty years older than me. He was bowlegged with an enormous belly. I stopped to ask him why he was at the event. He said he knew someone who'd had the disease and he feels terrible for what women with cancer go through. Wayne put a medal over my head and told me he lives two hours away and goes to different breast cancer events in costume and supports women who have had the disease. He shared his contact information with me, and we became friends on social media.

Wayne sent me a message a few months later. "There's a Strike Out Cancer minor league baseball game this summer. Do you want to go with me? Would you wear the breast cancer attire you wore to the mall walk?"

It sounded like fun. I'd never been to a league baseball game.

He shared he attends minor league baseball games often.

I mentioned it to Kevin, who didn't have a problem with me going. Wayne and I met on a Friday afternoon at a local gym in town. He was staying at a nearby motel. For safety, I made friends aware of my plans, and I shared my iPhone location with them. I parked my car at the gym, and Wayne and I rode to the game in his vehicle.

With Wayne being older, and me not knowing him, I hoped our conversation wouldn't be awkward. He had a way of making me feel comfortable. To ensure nothing worrisome happened, I mentioned Kevin and that we were seeing each other.

He asked, "Does he know you're with me?"

"Yes."

"Is Kevin threatened by me?"

"No." *Why would he be?*

Wayne told me he takes care of his elderly mother and still works part time. He wasn't sure how long she could live alone.

It was a muggy summer evening. The game was fun. There weren't many others in costume. I tried to decline, but he insisted on getting me a small baseball helmet filled with vanilla ice cream.

Our team won! After the game, he offered to buy me a baseball breast cancer jersey. I said, "Thank you, but I can't accept it." As we drove back to my vehicle, Wayne was interested in hearing my cancer story. I shared more about myself and my breast cancer. Wayne mentioned other survivors having shared many things, including photos with him, but he'd never seen a woman with her mastectomy scars.

Odd thing to tell me. But he's older… overlook it.

When we got back to my vehicle at the gym, it was late. At the car, Wayne presented me with a breast cancer swag bag and several breast cancer awareness shirts. After we got out of his vehicle, he wanted to hug me, and I allowed it, because he was just being friendly. I thanked him for taking me to the game. I was surprised when he held on to me a little too long, which was followed by a kiss on my cheek. *He's only being nice.* I pulled away from the hug and drove home.

I saw on one of Wayne's social media posts that his mother's ninety-fifth birthday was coming. In the post, he asked people to send her a birthday card. I thought, "That's a sweet thing for him to do for her. It's the least I could do." I picked up a birthday card for his mother and reached out to Wayne via text for her address. I mailed it in time for it to arrive before her birthday.

⚓

A lady I know was diagnosed with breast cancer. There was an upcoming "5K Fun Run," a fundraiser for breast cancer victims, and I joined her team to support her. Wayne reached out because it was breast cancer walk season, and he wanted to join me for the same 5K. As our last event had gone well, I didn't foresee a problem.

Wayne was staying at a different motel on the way to the 5K, and I offered to let him ride with me since he'd driven last time. It was a beautiful early fall morning. Because the weather was cooler, I wore a long-sleeved black and pink breast cancer shirt, black leggings with pink ribbons, and a hair buff. When I arrived at the motel, Wayne grabbed me for a hug and told me it had been sixty-four days since he'd seen me. He was wearing his pink costume. I told Wayne, "It's time to leave."

During our car trip, he mentioned there was a hockey fights cancer game in November and invited me. On the spot, I couldn't think of any other plans I had that day and agreed to go. "I'm glad," he said. "Will you wear your breast cancer event outfit?"

"Sure," I said. "I don't have any plans."

"Today, can we eat lunch at my favorite chain Italian restaurant after the Run? And keep our pink attire on?"

"I don't have a change of clothes with me anyway," I said.

After we parked, Wayne played his supporting part well. He gave swag bags out to women. He proudly showed me his phone's photo albums. He has four albums, one album for each breast cancer state's events and one album with photos of his favorite cancer survivors. He smiled when he showed me I was the key photo in the album for my state and also in his "favorites" album. It caught me off guard. Since the temperature was only in the upper 40s, I mentioned being chilly. Without asking permission, he wrapped his cape around me, pulled me in, and hugged me. He had to have felt my discomfort with him as stiffened and pulled away. Then, he surprised me by picking me up like he was carrying me across the threshold.

I said, "Put me down! I'm too heavy."

He did.

I was hoping he'd leave me alone. *How could a man who seemed twenty years older, with knee problems, pick me up like that?* It turned out he's just twelve years older than me. I'm not a lightweight, but he bowls often, so he's strong enough to lift a heavy ball.

Wayne thought I was younger than I am. *Could he have the wrong idea about this situation?* I reviewed our time together. I'd done nothing other than be nice to him.

"What are your plans in the coming weeks?" Wayne asked.

"I'm going on my first cruise soon," I said.

"I want to see your 'bikini pics.'"

I was caught by surprise. He was making assumptions, and I didn't like it. But he was riding back with me, and I avoid confrontation, unless I can't. Uncomfortable, I said, "I don't post bikini pics."

I walked for most of the event, and my finish time was barely over fifty minutes, which wasn't bad for my age. We left the event and drove to the restaurant. Wayne wore his pink clothing proudly—and I wondered if he did it just for attention. Wayne and the server were saying things to stroke my ego. They both talked about how pretty and shapely I was while being flirty. It made me uncomfortable, and my clairsentience flared up. I was surprised when Wayne told the server and me he'd move to the state I live in for me, but that he'd have to talk to his mom. She might move, too. I finished my lunch quickly and was about to pay my bill. I was taken aback to find that Wayne had already paid for the meal while I was in the restroom. He wouldn't accept payment from me.

I wanted to get back to the motel and drop him off. Returning to my car, I felt anxious. Thank goodness his motel was only ten minutes away, but as I drove there, it seemed longer. I said little on the way. I felt vulnerable about what had transpired.

When we arrived at the motel, I was relieved. As we said goodbye, Wayne stood too close to me—he was in my personal space. He hugged me again—for too long. He kissed my cheek.

I struggle with unwanted situations like this and was at a loss for words. It repelled me, but I didn't want to be impolite.

"Pack a bag for after the game if you want," Wayne said.

I felt sick to my stomach. *Let this be over.* Before I left, Wayne told me he was making a quilt out of breast cancer survivors' tee shirts, and would give it to an organization to auction off.

"Would you like to donate yours?" he asked.

As I left the motel, I said, "I will. Send me your mailing address."

He sent it to me via text.

Thinking about Wayne's words and actions the next day, my intuition kicked in. I keep most texts and found the address he'd given me for his mom—it was the same address as his. *He'd led me to believe he didn't live with his mother!* God was giving me a huge warning, even more than I'd felt previously.

I figured it out. Wayne was attentive to a very vulnerable group: cancer survivors. This was a tough pill to swallow. *I felt foolish. How many women has he treated this way—or has he?* The situation alarmed me. When I told Kevin what had transpired, he said he'd felt something was off with the situation all along.

He asked, "Am I going to have to kick an old man's ass?"

I replied, "No, that isn't necessary." Knowing I needed to wrap things up with Wayne with no loose ends, I sent him a text:

I mailed the tee shirt to you. When you mentioned the hockey game and packing a bag for after, I was taken aback. I've been seeing someone for several months. I'm happy and not interested in seeing anyone else. He hasn't minded me going to cancer events with you. I don't want to lead you on. I wanted to check and see if you'd rather invite someone else to the game instead of me. I wouldn't be going.

⚓

He replied, "No worries, I only thought about a bag, in case you'd want to change into regular clothes after the game for dinner. You're still invited to the game, and we'll grab an early dinner afterwards. I'm thrilled you have someone you're seeing, and that he isn't threatened by me."

Because of having been borderline stalked by Erick's wife (and having to go to court to get a restraining order), and because I'd feared Brian's anger when he didn't receive estate funds after Mama's death, I felt exposed. My safety comes first. No exceptions. I realized Wayne likely had my address from me having mailed his mother a birthday card. The following day, I created a Facebook post intended for his eyes only. "Things are hectic for me," I wrote, "and I'm taking a break from social media." After that, I blocked him on social media and on my phone.

I was independent. I thought nothing like this could happen to me. Thank God, nothing else happened. Kevin felt I should notify the breast cancer groups about the situation, so I sent messages to administrators of the groups and made posts on different pages, with a synopsis of what happened without giving his name or accusing him. After reading my post, a few breast cancer survivors became enraged. Many wanted me to out him, but I didn't.

After recognizing who he was, one admin responded, "I'm so sorry you were in those situations. Yes, his hugs are longer sometimes. I'm glad you shared."

I hadn't been violated, but I'd welcomed someone who'd felt like a predator into my life. I shouldn't have invited him in. He took advantage of my demeanor, and the situation could've ended badly. I'll maintain boundaries and be more aware of the hidden dangers in the future. Always listen to your intuition! It won't steer you wrong. I'm thankful that Divine protected me.

Chapter Fifteen

Hoping for Vulnerability

Kevin and Erick both stayed on my mind, but my thoughts of Kevin increased and gave me time to rest my mind from Erick taking up residence in my brain. My heart and mind were conflicted, but I made baby steps toward Kevin. I told Kevin there was something about his energy. I texted, "I'm a moth being drawn to your intense flame."

He replied: ❤.

We resumed our twenty questions game, and it was my turn. I wanted to nurture our connection. "What would it take for you to be vulnerable?"

Kevin said he didn't know. "It's where I've struggled the most," he said. "I'm afraid of being hurt. I don't think about it. I want to be vulnerable, but my shield goes up. I'm not sure I know how to even be vulnerable anymore."

The best answer he could give was, "Time."

If I hadn't told him about Erick, he would've had trust issues with me if he found out later.

It was Kevin's turn. He wanted me to describe my feelings for him. I started with vulnerability.

To say I have deep feelings doesn't convey what's inside of me. You bring me happiness and joy. I'm disappointed when we set dates and you have to work, and I struggle with wanting more time than you have for me. I'm unsure if you have it in you to make time for me. I want and need to be a priority. I could fall deeply in love with you and have peace and happiness in my heart. I'm scared of falling for you and you not feeling the same way.

Kevin validated me:

Awwww. Honey, I've been going to bed early every night. The heat takes its toll on me. I see a future for us, too. I'm looking forward to winter, when I have an abundance of free time. I want to spend as much time with you as possible.

"Kevin," I asked, "What's something you want to tell me, but haven't?"

I feel close to you, although we haven't spent a lot of time together. I think of you often and what our future would be. I think about how pretty you are and how much I love you and your smile. I think about how easily I could fall in love with you. There's little free time right now, but I'd like to spend more of what free time I have with you. I smile when I read your texts, and other people have commented on that. You check every box with what I want/need from a woman. I'm thrilled that we came into each other's lives.

This was huge and made me smile. I texted:
We haven't been around each other that much, but I've felt close to you. I don't have specific checkboxes, but my intuition (and heart) lets me know we're going to explore it. Do you believe we were brought into each other's lives randomly?

Kevin said, "Nothing about us feels random."

I texted back:

There's no random introduction of people into my life. I've sensed familiarity with you since you found me. I asked God to bring you into my life. People who come into my life since my awakening are from my past lives (for a higher purpose). My cards and pendulum show that we've been in each other's lives before.

He responded, "Hmmm."

The time had come for another movie and dinner date at a local steakhouse. I loved how Kevin was traditional in buying me a nice dinner and how we both loved movies. After our date, I texted, "When you touched my leg and my fingers, you set my body ablaze."

He said he'd felt the same energy.

My intuition continued to bother me. I laid out Tarot card spreads off and on, and they revealed the Three of Cups, meaning a third party's energy. Is it Cory or Jane? One day, Kevin told me he and Jane used to send links of songs to each other throughout the day, but they haven't done that in years. That day, Jane had sent him a Luke Bryan song, "Kiss Tomorrow Goodbye." Kevin had texted her back, asking, "Are you drunk?"

When I looked up the song's lyrics to discern its meaning, I realized Jane wanted to be intimate with Kevin.

He admitted, "It came out of left field."

Knowing Kevin still had a friendship with Cory and that their relationship had dissolved a year ago, I thought it was Cory that had alerted my intuition, but now I know the cards were cautioning me about Jane.

When I pressed Kevin with a few questions about Jane, he said, "Honey, you have nothing to worry about. Jane knows I'm seeing someone. Nothing's going to come of it," he said. He didn't want me to be jealous.

I told Kevin, "I know that, because of the things you've said about her. I'm not jealous… her sending the song was inconsiderate."

Kevin said Jane thinks mostly of herself. He thought that whomever she'd been seeing may have dumped her, since her sending the song was out of character for her.

With our chemistry, I stayed puzzled about Kevin's lack of physicality to me. He'd only ever kissed me. I felt he contained his emotions and held back. I messaged him, "Are you attracted to me in multiple ways? If you are, why haven't we done more than kiss?"

Kevin texted:

I'm attracted to you in every way. I told myself after my last relationship that I wouldn't have sex again unless I was in love in every way possible. I'm getting too old for that to be a primary focus for me. I want love. The rest will come. I'm growing close to you. I think about you all the time. I want to be sure that it's what I hope it is before I dive in. Sex is much more than sex for me. That connection is special, and I treat it as such. I know you're eager, and I appreciate your patience. I need to know that I won't get hurt again.

Again, I tried to ease his fear of vulnerability and having a relationship with me. He'd put my mind at ease.

Both Erick and Kevin were in my thoughts, and I remained conflicted. Kevin was the first man I truly wanted to move forward with after Erick. *But could I?* I've loved since Erick, but with Kevin, it was different. I had a serious case of "the feels." Although I was healing, my cards kept showing a third-party energy. With both of us having anxiety, I didn't want to fall into my same patterns from the past.

I knew my broken heart was ready to love again but was scared. The glue that had held it together after Erick was still damp. Kevin's availability was limited. He works fourteen hours a day, six days a week, sometimes more. Knowing his kids and work come first, I struggled with what little time we spent together, but my patience remained. Since I'd worked similar hours in the past, I understood it better than most people would.

Kevin treated me the way a man should treat a woman. Sometimes, Jeremy's schedule changed or David was sick, so I tried not to be disappointed when we rescheduled dates. It was hard, though. I wanted to spend more time with him. His energy was addictive, and that's how I know there's a genuine connection. Yes, I was falling… falling hard.

Chapter Sixteen

Manifesting and Protecting

It was a hot, sunny morning, a few weeks after the incident with Wayne, and I was finishing my walk on the greenway. There were many trees on both sides of the paved greenway. As always, I prayed for Erick near the end of my walk. For a long time, I prayed for us to be brought together, that we'd talk to one another in person, and that we'd speak our minds without ego, fear, pride, or anyone interrupting us. One moment, I was praying for him, and then... *OMG!* He was walking toward me.

I did a double take. We met near the Grandfather tree, where I ground myself most days. My hair was in a tortoise-shell clip, pulled off my face, and I was wearing a green tank top and grey volleyball shorts. I was thirty pounds lighter than when I'd seen him on New Year's Eve over two years earlier. He wore baggy black and white shorts and a tee shirt, and was about three feet to my left.

"Erick," I said.

He looked at me. I removed my oversized tortoise-shell sunglasses. A look of disbelief came over his face, and instantly, his green eyes softened, as if he were in deep thought. I wish I'd known what he was thinking. He acted like he was glad to see me. I'm not sure who was more surprised.

He looked me in the eye and then down at my body, stopping at my abdomen.

He's checking to see if I still have boobs after my cancer.

He seemed to approve of my new outer shell. He smiled. "You look good."

I said, "Thank you. Do you walk here?"

No one was around. Erick seemed more relaxed and replied, "It's my first morning."

"I moved to my HOA complex three years ago," I said, pointing in that direction. I mentioned it, hoping he wouldn't bring Karen to Jeff's place. It would be awful if she saw me.

"How are you?" he asked gently.

Upbeat and smiling, I said, "I'm good. How are you?"

I couldn't believe it when he looked me in the eye and admitted, "I've been through hell."

I know you have.

Seeing how he was being honest, my smile faded. I let my face relax. My eyes penetrated his green eyes, and I allowed my innermost emotions to show. "Me too," I replied.

He said something else I can't recall, but I sensed he feared that if anyone saw us together, they'd report back to Karen. We parted ways.

Why can't I remember our last words? They weren't anything life altering. As I was walking away, I realized Erick hadn't had the same effect on me he'd had in the past. I felt positive. Adrenaline was pumping through my body, so I stayed at the Grandfather tree to ground. I realized over time, I'd visualized seeing him there many days—and I'd manifested his presence. Everyone has this ability. You think about what you desire, focus on it, and see it in your third eye. (Try it and see what happens!)

Manifestation

Another extension of this approach is manifesting during a new moon cycle. A new moon phase is the first phase of a moon's cycle, when the moon is between the Earth and the Sun, which makes the moon's surface appear dark. During the full moon, it's time to release what burdens you. You can ask for multiple items. I write on paper what I want to manifest or release and go outside with a clear Mason jar and a lighter. I look up at the sky at night and say my intentions out loud. Then I fold the paper up like it's a fan, tuck it into the jar, and burn it. After the paper has a few charred remains and has cooled off, I either blow the ashes out of the jar onto the grass or take them to the nearby lake and let them fall into the water.

Psychic Clarity

It had been a month since Kevin had shared with me that Jane wanted to have casual sex with him and Cory wanted to come see him. After I got home, I texted Kevin and told him I'd seen Erick. "We spoke, but that was all. Nothing more," I wrote. I told him what Erick had said about being through hell. Also, I told him I'd mentioned to Erick where I lived, so he wouldn't drive with Karen to Jeff's. I felt nervous about her seeing me. When he responded several hours later, he didn't ask me about it.

He'll ask me more in person, I thought.

That same afternoon, I spoke with Sylvia, a trusted medium. Many people think psychic readings are of the devil or that they aren't accurate. I've been fortunate to work with great Tarot card readers, wonderful psychics, and mediums who have provided truths, and they've helped me develop my psychic abilities and give others accurate information.

I told Sylvia, a fellow twin, "I saw and spoke with Erick, my Twin Flame, while walking today on the greenway."

Sylvia said, "You triggered Erick. He gravitated toward your energy."

I listened and reclined in my brown leather chair. "We saw each other near the tree I ground at daily," I said. "I'm so glad I wasn't triggered. I pray for him each morning."

"Seeing you brought back how he's felt about you the entire time, and he feels so much love. It was natural for him to tell you the truth about the hell he's gone through."

I swallowed. "We've both been through hell."

"Things are turbulent for Erick in his home life. He knows he no longer has power over you. There was an energetic exchange between you both when you spoke. He was confused, because until then, he'd thought he'd done work on himself. But when he saw you, all that went out the window."

"I've healed more," I said. "I felt unbalanced after seeing him."

"There was no egoic energy between you. It's as though Erick had seen you as someone who'd healed from sickness. He knows now you were both to blame for the affair, not just you."

"I tried to walk away five times, but he didn't let me go until Karen found out about the affair." *Did he ever admit his part of that to Karen?*

"Erick's still being controlled, and his marriage isn't the same." Sylvia felt Karen was with Erick when he's out, and it's beyond coincidence that we'd seen each other without her being with him.

Health Crisis

That evening, I drove to a new friend's home for dinner. Sadie had introduced me to Kimber after my breakup with Larry.

Kimber has a tan skin tone and chestnut hair. She and I are the same age. Kimber has experienced life difficulties, and she's a recovering alcoholic. I respect her openness about her addiction.

After I did a Tarot reading for her roommate, we ate Kimber's steak dinner. I haven't eaten steak in several years. After visiting with her, I returned home that night. My hands were itchy, reminiscent of earlier this summer when I'd had to go to urgent care for an unknown allergic reaction. I went to bed and ignored it.

At 1:30 a.m., I woke up. My hands were super itchy, and the white jersey knit sheet was painful against my skin. *Why does it hurt?* I got up, turned the light on, and looked at myself in the mirror: red hives covered my body from head to toe. There were even some on my scalp. *Oh crap, an allergic reaction.* Realizing I was in impending danger, I grabbed my phone off the nightstand. Summer, a friend who had taken care of me after my mommy-makeover surgery, had texted me after 1:00 a.m.

I texted her and asked, "Are you still awake?"

"Yes, I'm watching a movie."

Oh thank God. She can talk to me. My heart was racing, and I was pacing. I called her. "I'm covered with hives," I said. "I think I'm having an allergic reaction to something."

"Go to the hospital now."

"Yes. I am."

I kept Summer on speakerphone as I put shorts and a tee shirt on and drove myself to the local Emergency Department. I tried to drive the speed limit and arrived there in under ten minutes. After hanging up from Summer, I hurried inside the automatic doors.

They triaged me quickly. As the male nurse took my information, my heart rate and blood pressure were high. My blood pressure averages 96/66. It was 150/120 because I was scared. The nurse started an IV. I watched my vital signs on the monitor. They gave me a shot of Benadryl through the IV. I told the nurse I wasn't breathing well. My ear canals felt swollen, and my hearing was muffled. Upon checking my throat, he said, "It's closing." Panic overcame me.

The nurse left to find a doctor. *What's happening to me?* I took a photo of myself—my face was so swollen; there were no wrinkles. The doctor came in and said, "You're having an allergic reaction. We're going to give you a shot of epinephrine."

The nurse squeezed my upper thigh and administered epinephrine. It worked, and as I rested in the narrow hospital bed, my breathing returned to normal. Within an hour, I was discharged. The hives had started to fade before I left.

I drove home and went to sleep. I awoke mid-morning, and there were no hives remaining. You would've thought that nothing had been wrong with me six hours earlier.

Three months earlier, I'd been bitten by a Lone Star tick, which has a white spot on its back. Lone Star tick bites can cause a red meat allergy called Alpha-gal syndrome. That tick was on me for three days before I found it. A woman I'd once worked with told me she had an allergy to meat. Remembering what she'd said tipped me off to be allergy tested—*I'd had steak at Kimber's and I'd been bitten by a tick. Did I have an allergic reaction to it?* I realized this was a second, more dangerous reaction than the one I'd had two months earlier when I'd eaten a hamburger. I could've died. All of this motivated me to find out what had caused the reaction.

A few weeks later, I saw an allergist and received a definitive diagnosis confirmed with lab work. My lab work showed I had high levels of IgE in my blood, and showed I was positive for Alpha-gal syndrome. It's an allergy to mammalian meat, and means I can no longer eat pork, beef, lamb, or goat meat—or any animal that has been nursed by its mama. I'll have my bloodwork drawn again in a few years to see if I remain diagnosis positive. I miss hamburger, bacon, and ribs the most; however, I've found turkey bacon and a vegetarian burger I can tolerate. After my diagnosis, I only eat chicken, turkey, and seafood.

What I learned through this experience is that your health can change in the blink of an eye. I realized it may not have been such a good idea to drive myself to the hospital. I could've gone into anaphylaxis and caused an accident—or I could've stopped breathing and no one who found me would've known why. I could've died. Living alone, I can't ignore things and hope for the best. My time here could've been over, yet I know there are things I still need to do. Once again, I acknowledged I'd been protected by Divine.

Chapter Seventeen

Hearing Three Little Words

When I cooked for Kevin for the first time, it had been five months since he'd found me on Facebook's dating app, and two months since our first date. I lack cooking skills, but I tried for the first time to prepare manicotti with my thirty-five-year-old homemade spaghetti sauce recipe. It turned out perfectly. He loved it, and it turned out we both love bread and chocolate cake, too.

After our bellies were full, we went to a movie. The armrests in the theater are adjustable, so we cuddled. Kevin laid his hand on my upper thigh. His touch gave me chills. After it was over, we walked outside. He lit a cigarette, and I sat on a grassy area close to him.

Puffing on his cigarette, Kevin mentioned, "You saw Erick on the greenway."

"Yes, I did. It shocked me seeing him."

I gave Kevin casual details of me having seen Erick, because after his reaction (thinking Luke was Erick), I didn't want him to worry. He knew Jeff lived on my street and how I'd struggled with knowing that. Kevin seemed accepting of this. He extinguished his cigarette. We walked back to my vehicle, and he drove to his place. Later, after Kevin left, I thought, "It's a slippery slope when you love two men." Although I cared for Erick, I knew Kevin was helping me release him. I was working on myself and praying my heart would transition and belong to Kevin.

He texted when he got home. "I loved our beautiful evening together."

Kevin knew my darkest secrets, and he accepted me for who I am. Some people wouldn't love a recovering alcoholic or addict, but he's so irresistible. I couldn't help myself. Kevin worked hard to remain sober, and I respected him for his honesty. Mutual acceptance and respect were big parts of who we were. Not all men would accept someone with a history of cancer, but it didn't seem to faze Kevin.

Having had two surgeries in nine months, I have fears when intimacy is a possibility. *How will a man react to my scars?* After my breast reduction/lift and full abdominoplasty, twenty staples were removed. With the lumpectomy site, the lymph node removal area, and the scar from the radiation-delivery catheter device, I'm scarred more than most people. Some scars have faded with the scar removing gel I used, but I'll always have them. Only Larry has seen me before and after both surgeries. He saw all my scars, and they didn't seem to bother him. When I shared details of my scars with Kevin, I wasn't sure what his reaction would be.

He texted, "Those scars are reminders you're a survivor and fortunate to have them."

"I know I am, but I have some insecurity about my scarring."

When he told me I was an inspiration to him, I smiled. Being a recovering alcoholic and sharing his own story with others also encouraged me. I felt closer to him.

Birthday

There were times I sensed Kevin was thinking of me. It was the intuitive feeling I've had with Erick before. One day, he sent me a strange phrase I figured out was a song lyric. Kevin said we were "in sync."

I smiled when Kevin started sending songs to me through text. He sent me Blake Shelton songs, which made me happy. My favorite one was "God Gave Me You."

"How do you feel about me, Kevin?"

"I like you more than I've liked any woman in a long time. Sometimes that scares me."

I wanted to hug him. "Know you're safe with me."

"The more I know you, the more comfortable I am with the idea you won't hurt me."

When Kevin said he has never dumped anyone in his life, it surprised me. "It's always mutual," he said, "or she left. I'm cautious about who I'm involved with, because once I'm involved, I'm loyal... sometimes to a fault. I've experienced hurt, sometimes worse than others. I guard my heart, but once I open up, I do it knowing I could be hurt. It's the biggest reason I take things slowly."

Kevin cares, and his inability to spend as much time with me as he wants to had nothing to do with me.

One thing Kevin isn't good at is remembering dates. I told him a couple of months ago my birthday was September 11. My fifty-fourth birthday arrived, and I'd hoped he would remember. Most women want gifts and other gestures, but not me—a "Happy Birthday" is sufficient. But by mid-morning, he hadn't wished me a happy birthday. I was hurt. My 9/11 birthday used to be a normal day, but when people asked for my birthday after our nation's tragedy, when learning my birthdate, they'd often say "I'm sorry."

I sent a text to Kevin:

I'm hurt you didn't wish me a happy birthday. It makes me question if you can give me more. I don't want to be just a convenient thought or accept breadcrumbs—it's a pattern I keep repeating.

Despite limited time together, there's strong closeness between us. Our conversations stimulate me, and I've fallen in love with you. Your kindness has chipped away at the wall I built after my affair, letting you into my guarded, broken heart. You're helping me mend it. When I love, I love deeply, but I have continual anxiety about this.

We both have wounds. I want to be with you in all ways and hope you feel the same. As I get older, I'm gaining clarity on what I can and can't accept. I discount my feelings and put others first. I want someone who will meet me halfway with effort and invest their time in me.

Kevin responded:

I'm so sorry! I'm terrible at remembering dates—it's one of my worst qualities. I want you to understand why I seem distracted or distant, but it has nothing to do with my feelings for you. I need to explain this face to face, not through text. There's pain I'm learning to deal with, and I'm not good at opening up.

Women have said these exact words to me before. I've dealt with a lot too and can explain, but only in person. I think about you all day, every day. I don't have time to text as much as I'd like, but you're always on my mind. I've fallen in love

with you too, which is hard for reasons I'll explain. Let's plan
an evening for you to come over, meet Jeremy, and have dinner.
Happy birthday—sorry I missed it. ❤️

A week later, after his family had all gotten over COVID-19, Kevin invited me to his home for the first time. He'd bought his dad's ranch-style home years ago, and he referred to it as "the bachelor pad." It was comfortable, and I noticed his appreciation of dark, antique furniture. Meeting Jeremy was an enjoyable experience—he radiated kindness and respect. Jeremy and Kevin have a close bond.

I got to meet Jeremy's young bearded dragon, Abby. Jeremy brought her out to meet me. I touched her briefly, but I don't like holding reptiles, so I didn't pick her up. Abby seemed to know her name. Jeremy proudly showed me her environment—an immaculate aquarium with a warming light. He showed me how he feeds her crickets.

After dinner, Kevin asked me to wait with the door closed in his bedroom. It was a typical man's room, comfortable. I realized I'd seen his sleigh bed before—through my third eye. My book was on his dresser. He gave me the "Okay" to come out to the kitchen. I was delighted to see a yummy chocolate cake with lit candles. *Awww.* When I tried to blow them out, they relit. Ha! Kevin also gave me a beautiful mum with multi-colored blossoms and purple shoots.

I didn't mind my birthday being delayed, as long as it was remembered. Kevin and I went into his bedroom, and I hugged him. Nervous, I whispered those three little words, "I love you," in his ear as we hugged, and he said, "I love you, too." I sighed, and a sweet kiss followed. *I felt happy and special.*

Evening Walk

A few days later, Kevin came over for dinner. After we ate, he asked, "Will you walk with me on the greenway?"

It was early fall, and the temperatures were cooler after dark, so he wore my grey Smashing Pumpkins sweatshirt. Having him walk with me at the same place I walk most mornings felt good. We talked, and he held my hand as we walked. It was a clear night, and the leaves had turned vibrant red and orange.

He told me he's in therapy. I felt walking makes it easier for him to express his feelings. Kevin said, "I shared one of your texts with Cory."

My anxiety crept up. I'd told him about the Tarot card spread I'd laid, and how I'd worried about his feelings for Cory. He said that after he'd shared one of my texts with her, she'd said she liked me (through my words) and said I knew how to express my feelings healthily.

We talked about Jane. "She's a narcissist," he said. Kevin is old-fashioned and thinks people are too quick to resort to divorce. It's hard for him, he told me, to envision ever being married again.

My intuition about Jane kept bugging me earlier that week, so I'd laid Jane's cards. I don't like surprises, which is why I check into others' energies. I discovered she still had feelings for Kevin, and I'd told him so. "I don't have feelings for her." he'd said. "I feel sick when I think about getting back together with her."

I didn't think I had anything to worry about. Jane had cheated on him once, and he told me he didn't want to be intimate with her anymore. They had separated a year after the affair and later, got back together to cut expenses for two homes. They had lived together until three years ago, but their divorce was only completed two months before he found me.

When Kevin told me Erick was the one pause he had toward me, I asked him not to pause. He was experiencing depression, which he said occurs for him in the fall.

We walked back to my place after dark, and he gave my sweatshirt back. After that conversation on the greenway, my worry over Jane lessened. I felt relieved and happy. His scent was in my sweatshirt, and I slept with it until I couldn't smell him anymore.

A week later, I cooked dinner for Kevin at his place on his white stove. I knew something was off—he was distant most of the evening. He didn't sit beside me as he normally did. When we hugged goodbye, he didn't kiss me or tell me he loved me.

What's going on?

He thanked me for coming over and said he'd enjoyed my company. He'd said he'd open up about his depression but needed time to process the root cause. He was trying to work through it in his brain. He said he appreciated me not pushing for answers right now and wasn't prepared to explain it yet.

When he texted me the next morning, he wanted to share something with me. He sent a song that might help explain his depression. It was a sad song about leaving. When he texted, "I don't know how to say this…," a pit formed in my stomach. I thought I was going to vomit.

I insisted he say it.

"I really like you. That's why this is a struggle. I'm not good for anyone right now, and it's not fair to ask you to wait for me. I'm still in love with Jane. It doesn't matter because it will go nowhere, but until I can get over this, I can't ask you to wait. I'm sorry. I don't want to feel the way I do, but I can't deny it either."

It felt like I was having an out-of-body experience. My world was imploding.

I was confused, hurt, and angry. "Why did you tell me you weren't in love with her? Why didn't you tell me this last night? Why did you tell me you loved me and now you 'like me'? I don't know what to say."

He said, "I told you the ship has sailed… and it has. She and I can't be together for many reasons, but I must figure out how to heal. I'm working on it with therapy, but I'm not there yet. I'm sorry. I have to be honest."

Kevin didn't want me to disappear from his life because, he said, I'm an amazing person and deserve to be loved by someone who isn't depressed and trapped in the past. He wished he could be that guy right now.

"I wish you could, too. You shouldn't have told me you loved me. I felt safe with you. You lied. The Tarot card spreads I've laid about Jane don't lie. I still love Erick, but I was ready to move forward with you.

He replied, "I know you are." Kevin didn't want me to cut him out of my life altogether. He knew he'd hurt me, yet said he didn't want to be without me in his life. I was special to him.

Even though I said, "I don't plan on disappearing," I felt my boundaries going up. I was retreating into my safe inner world for protection. I was shell-shocked. A full trigger was coming, and I couldn't stop it. "When I questioned things about you and Jane," I said, "you reassured me."

Knowing that Kevin, Jane, Jeremy, and David were going to a fall festival together, as they always do, I asked one thing of him. "If you post pictures on Facebook, block me so I don't have to see it." I wanted to know, "Did you ever love me?"

Kevin said, "I love you, and that's why I couldn't drag you through this. It's not fair to you."

I'd trusted him, blindly. Love or like, my heart was breaking… again.

He told me, "I need time to be alone and clear my head. I don't want to see anyone else. I wanted you to have the opportunity if that's what you want. I need a friend more than anything else right now. I hope you understand."

Because he's a Libra, I already know that they retreat and you let them be. When my world is chaotic and I'm rejected,

I retreat into my inner shell and put up protective barriers. It can be a scary place.

This trigger was like ones I've experienced when Erick rejected and abandoned me. Seeing photos from the fall festival a few days later, there was one of Jane on Kevin's Facebook page, which hurt me and triggered horrendous anxiety. It looked like they'd had a good time. *They're reuniting.* I couldn't take seeing it, so I unfriended and blocked him on Facebook. I'd asked one thing of him—to block me from seeing those posts—and it was as if he'd slapped my face. I couldn't stomach it.

Right before this, I ordered Kevin a three-year sobriety coin before our breakup. "Never give in. Three years. Your sobriety is a big deal. I love you and I'm proud of you." I mailed it to him. I wished him a Happy Sobriety Birthday on October 17.

Elohee was coming soon. Thank God! *My respite and safe space.*

Kevin's fiftieth birthday was almost here, and I'd already purchased a customized, light-emitting diode (LED) clear sign with his company logo with a man pushing a mower on it. I wanted him to have it, along with his birthday card, so I decided to drop it off on my way to Elohee.

Traffic was heavy that beautiful October morning as I drove through into our state's capital. I stopped at Kevin's and left his gift on the porch. It was gut-wrenching for me to pull into his driveway and park. I was sad.

Kevin got my letter in the mail. He texted me after receiving it to say he cared about me, and it had never been his intention to hurt me, but he'd wanted to be open and honest. His life was confusing right now. "I'm sorry," he said. "I hope we can remain friends and see where it goes, but I understood you might not do that." Thankful for the AA chip and light, he said, "You're an amazing person. I don't deserve you right now."

He's with Jane… I must accept that.

When I arrived at Elohee, I was a mess the first day. However, I knew it was time to write again. Some of the best writing I do comes when I'm heartbroken. While I had avoided writing for several months, by the time I left Elohee, I'd written some. The healing that happens on that land is life changing. Whereas I used to be a joiner on many activities, while there, I pulled back, stayed on my own, and wrote.

After returning home three weeks after Kevin walked away, I looked at my phone.

Kevin texted, "Hi. I see you blocked me on Facebook. Don't know if you blocked my cell number. Did you have a happy Halloween?"

I was shocked when I saw his message. "I went to a Halloween party over the weekend. I didn't block you for the reason you may think."

Kevin said he missed talking to me.

I missed him, too. I asked, "Have you been working on yourself?"

He texted, *With my therapist, I've worked through much of it. The difference is I've been doing the recommended work, which I haven't done in the past. I've been in a sad place for a long time and thought if I could quit drinking, all my problems would go away. Many did, but years of drinking also left me with scars that are still healing.*

Kevin had expected the storybook ending if he put the bottle down and thought that pieces would fall into place. When that didn't turn out, he didn't know what to do, and he went through daily life without direction. His only fulfillment came from Jeremy and David. Kevin had become hyper-independent and wasn't willing to be vulnerable.

He also said that work had slowed, which gave him time to focus. His therapist had given him tools to work with. Saying he'd only posted pictures of the kids on Facebook, Kevin claimed he was trying to be sensitive, knowing I didn't want to see pictures of Jane—or him, for that matter.

I texted, "No, you posted one photo with Jane in it. Where are you at in your feelings toward her... and me?"

When he hadn't responded by the following morning, I was angry.

I texted, "No answer is an answer." Although the first lyric of the song wasn't our situation, I sent a Little Rivers Band song that seemed fitting, "Take It Easy On Me."

Kevin replied to my text instantly. He said he'd never received my earlier text and that he'd understood my emotions with the song I sent. His feelings for me hadn't changed, and he was letting go of his feelings for Jane.

I reread it twice, and my heart was hopeful.

Kevin said he wanted to be with me but that I needed to understand that he had to release his feelings. He said he wasn't a bad guy and that he'd kept a respectable line drawn. Kevin hadn't slept with me, though he said he'd wanted to. He hadn't seen me as often as he'd wanted, and he'd done those things because he'd been trying to clear his head and didn't want to hurt me. He said it would've been easy to dive in and take what he wanted, but knowing how he felt, he couldn't. It wasn't fair to me because he cared for me.

It was time for my truth. When he admitted to living in the past, it triggered me. I texted:

I've always given more than I receive from partners and discounted myself. Knowing you're divorced, I believed you. What I see now is that when I've asked uncomfortable questions, you often sidestepped the answer. My cards showed you were deceptive, and I ignored my intuition.

"I'm 'deceptive'?! You're right. I took everything I wanted and lied to you. Seriously?! I'm deceptive because I was more honest than you wanted me to be."

Choice words came to my mind with his sarcasm.

It's what the cards had shown. I responded:

You were deceptive when I asked about your feelings toward Jane. Most men can't give me what I seek, but you do. Ninety-nine percent of men aren't what I'm attracted to beyond looks. You presented it differently from just "getting over my ex-wife." You wanted to make sure what we had was love. I ignored my intuition each time—that's on me. I'm angry, and it caused me to give more than you did.

When presented with the truth, Kevin clams up. He didn't defend or accept responsibility for what I'd texted. When he texted back, all he said was that he'd seen his first shooting star, a green one. Green is related to the heart chakra. It felt like he was healing in therapy, which gave me hope.

I started packing for my first cruise.

Chapter Eighteen

Reuniting

My first Caribbean cruise on the Allure of the Seas was in early November. The ship sailed from Port Canaval in Orlando. A house band performing reggae music on deck and ocean waves gently rocking the ship brought a peaceful rhythm to my ears. I found the walking track and logged several miles each day. There's nothing like toking on a ship's balcony at night, under a clear, starry sky, surrounded by the smell of the ocean and the roar of crashing waves. It's a special spiritual connection

When the ship docked in the Bahamas, I'd never seen water so transparent, a beautiful shade of turquoise. I loved hearing the Bahamians' native accent. While there, I had my hair braided. It was painful when the braider pulled the braids tight against my scalp. Later, I had a facial and a relaxing massage.

One night, as I sat on a balcony, I saw something supernatural. I looked up at the sky and saw a white object moving across it. It looked like an angel with wings. It had a white trail, and its head was brighter than its body. I captured it on video as it disappeared and reappeared. Later, I checked: no rockets had been launched that night from the Orlando area. When I showed the video to senior crew members, they told me I'd been blessed to have seen it.

During the cruise, Kevin and I communicated via text. He told me he's been working on clearing his head and said, "I can think straight for the first time in years."

Getting Back Together

After I returned from my cruise, Kevin asked me to dinner. I agreed. We met at a casual restaurant. I wore jeans and a pastel sweatshirt I'd bought in Coco Cay, a cruise destination. When I saw him inside the restaurant, butterflies were fluttering in my stomach. He was wearing a red and blue shirt and faded jeans and looked especially handsome. It was good to see him. I'd bought him a ball cap in Coco Cay and a Bahamas magnet, souvenirs from my cruise. While we ate, we caught up. I knew our "real" conversation was about to begin.

Kevin went into detail about his therapist and Jane. During therapy, when he'd realized he still loved Jane, the therapist said, "You have to tell her." Kevin went to her home and told her he needed to tell her something, and that he didn't want her to say anything. He told her and left.

He said he was sure Jane's ego was stroked. "I felt freer than I have in years," he said. When he'd signed up on the dating app, he said, he hadn't been in the right frame of mind.

This was a mirroring situation for me. I'd joined the dating app before I'd healed from Larry. I was taken aback when he said there would be no more hugs between him and Jane, because, he said, Jane uses hugs to her own advantage.

Why did he let Jane hug him and not stop it?

"I understand. I'm still getting over Erick. I know how hard it is. When everything between us broke down, I didn't know if I could ever trust another man," I said.

We went outside after dinner and sat in my car. We talked more, and we both accepted where things were. We made a fresh start and reunited.

Later, via text, I told Kevin I was releasing Erick more and was allowing Kevin into places inside my heart where only Erick has been.

He wanted to know more.

"It's hard to put into words. Parts of Erick I've kept guarded and protected within my mind and heart. They can't remain there, and I'm purging. You and your essence are filling spaces I never thought I'd let go of, because your energy has left its mark on me. That has only happened with Erick, so that's why I know you're different."

I wanted to spend Thanksgiving with Kevin and asked him what his plans were. My anxiety increased when he said Wendy, David, and Jane were coming over. My ego reared its ugly head. Since we're back together, I'd thought we'd spend our first major holiday together. I asked, "How am I supposed to feel knowing you'll spend Thanksgiving with her?"

He reminded me they spend holidays together for David's stability. Although I understood, still, I didn't like it.

"We can look at changing the way things are done from now on," Kevin texted, "but for this year at least, it's what he expects. It's all he's ever known. We watch the Lions play football each year. David's big on traditions."

Despite my willingness to embrace Jane going to Kevin's for the holiday, this unsettled me. But parenting has evolved since my parents' divorce. It didn't stop me from saying something I shouldn't: "How would you feel if I told you I was going to be around Erick? I'm not mad, but we need to discuss situations more. If you're involved with someone, that's who you want to spend holidays with."

He texted back: "Jane had asked me if she was still coming over for Thanksgiving, as her family was hundreds of miles away."

Knowing that, I settled down. No one should have to spend holidays alone. Until recently, we weren't talking to each other, much less about Thanksgiving. He reassured me he only wanted to be with me. "This isn't about Jane… in the least."

It seems that way.

When he reminded me that there had been no involvement between them in years, I reminded him they'd been hugging. Kevin asked me to stop and trust his intentions. I didn't want to argue. But it was fair for me to say what I thought. Recognizing David needed the consistency of both his parents, I knew I had to let it go.

When Kevin said he wasn't against starting new traditions, I was hopeful.

When I pray about situations that burden me, when my wounding is heightened and anxiety is overwhelming, it takes three days for my mind to quit racing and my nervous system to calm. The conflict in my mind is terrible. Knowing I wanted to give myself to Kevin and him alone, I talked to God. I told Him I didn't know how to let Erick go, but I knew I wanted and needed to. Saying this made my anxiety increase. My heart was being squeezed. My biggest truth was that this was the first time I'd asked for this in earnest. In the past, I'd asked, but didn't mean it. I begged God to pull the immense grief from my heart and to allow me to let Kevin fill those places that only Erick has occupied within me.

Painful tears exploded. God knows my heart and what's best for me. God also knew what I'd asked for felt impossible for me, and that releasing Erick from my heart would never happen. Although I've never experienced something happening immediately, I was shocked. There was an instant difference.

My tears stopped. This release isn't a one-size-fits-all situation, but I knew things were changing positively. God had answered my prayer.

I shared this with Kevin. "You're worth all the work. I'm not doing it just for you."

"That's fantastic!" Kevin said. "God definitely hears us."

One Friday night in early December, Kevin and I got takeout. It was a month after he returned to my life after our break. We drove to The Corner Cafe. Going in there no longer triggers me.

While driving, Kevin told me that there was something he needed to tell me in full honesty.

When he said this, I knew it involved Jane. I was glad to be driving in the dark so my emotions wouldn't show.

His therapist had guided him to tell Jane his feelings, which he'd done. Now, this morning, Jane had sent him an email highlighting their every problem and sharing the reasons they're divorced. He'd texted back, "You overlook the fact that you had an affair. My feelings for you almost cost me the best thing that has ever happened to me."

Me.

I was relieved he was moving on from her toward me. Kevin seemed resolved in his decision to not go back to her.

I asked how he'd met Jane.

He revealed that Tara and Jane were best friends.

What?!

Jane is an esthetician and used to give Tara, Kevin's first wife, facials in their home. Kevin had never met her. Jane had come by the house at the end of their marriage, and his then-roommate told her Tara had moved out. Later that day, Jane left zoo passes for Kevin and Jeremy in the mailbox. She called him the next day and asked if Kevin and Jeremy would go to the zoo with her. They did. Within two weeks, Kevin and Jane were living together.

Jane wanted to have a baby with Kevin a couple years later. He'd had concerns, as they were both nearing forty. Within three weeks, there was a positive pregnancy test. While she was pregnant with David, Kevin said she begged him to marry her. He did.

Kevin said that each week, he put $1,000 in an in-home emergency fund. By the following week, all the money was gone. He never asked Jane where the money went. I can't imagine how she spent that much money each week.

Kevin said that when he was married to both his wives, he was a pushover.

I'm paying the price for their actions.

Quiet Night at Home

That same night, our dinner was delicious, and the evening was lovely. We didn't have to be doing anything and enjoyed each other's company. We watched a comedy show on TV while sitting on the loveseat. As always, Kevin was too respectful.

I'd told him several times on past dates I loved him but decided I wouldn't say it again unless he said it again first. Before he left, we hugged at my kitchen island, and he said, "I do love you." I intuitively knew that Kevin loved me. Through our tight embrace, I felt his passion for me at that moment physically, which made me happy. I mustered my courage and asked a burning question. I didn't think how to ask, the words just spilled out: "When can we have sex?"

Kevin said he wanted to make sure all the pieces were as they should be—and we both knew they were. He wanted things to be perfect for our first time and feared being vulnerable. I whispered into his left ear, "I want you to. I want you to. I want you to." I hoped his stone wall was coming down.

Because of my experiences with men, plus Erick having once said, "It's all the same" when I asked him to "make love" to me, I can't say those words, although that's what I wanted.

I told Kevin, "Quit handling me with kid gloves." The love and desire I have for him is all-encompassing, and I wanted him to make love to me. I wanted him to look deep into my eyes and for us to connect on a magical level. As usual, Kevin listened and was receptive. He let my words sink in. We said our goodbye, and he drove home.

After Kevin got home that night, he texted me and thanked me for a nice evening.

I texted him and said, "It was a lovely evening. We're satisfied with being in each other's company. My heart loves you. I want intimacy with you in all ways. I know it's scary, but I'm going to use some of your words… trust my intentions."

He replied: ♥

After I'd contemplated, I texted:

We're imperfect people. There's a deep longing for you, sexually and otherwise. Your essence is something I can't put into words. It's an energetic pull toward you. I know you have a successful business, but that isn't on my radar when I think of you. You're an intelligent man… I'm drawn to your brain as I am to your physical features. I could lie with you and be content with that, too.

Kevin said, "It's so nice to wake up to your text."

Chapter Nineteen

Remembering (Past Life Regression)

Spending time on social media is a daily habit for me. Sometimes reels show up out of nowhere that hit close to home. One week, when I was still unaware of the term "anxious attachment," there were many reels in my feed about the subject. As I listened to therapists talk about this attachment style, I understood why the situation with Kevin had triggered me. There are four attachment styles, including:

1) Secure attachment: trusting and being comfortable within a relationship,
2) Dismissive avoidant attachment: desire for independence while not needing others,
3) Fearful-avoidant attachment: wanting intimacy but fearing closeness,
4) Anxious attachment: a deep desire for intimacy coupled with self-doubt and abandonment anxiety.

One day, I asked Kevin, "Besides algorithms, do you think some reels pop up in your social media feed randomly, or for other reasons?"

He replied, "Some seem too coincidental."

"I agree. I've discovered from reading a few posts that popped up on my feed that I have anxious attachment. I feel shame. For me, at that moment, it's like the end of the world. Irrational thoughts and anxiety paralyze me. I don't want to be this way."

Kevin said he thinks that sometimes, I expect the worst. He said he played a role in that and apologized. He thinks most people our age have some anxiety.

It's been six years since I've taken anxiety medication. Abandonment and rejection issues cause most of my anxiety, but as an empath, sizable crowds can feel overwhelming. Also, since I was a child, I've been afraid of storms.

Dangerous Weather

One December day, weather reports showed a tornado was coming. Sheets of rain and strong winds beat down on my townhome. When the winds picked up, I took Crystal and two things into my interior bedroom closet: bottled water for us and my vape pen. I knew having my vape pen would calm my nerves. As I noted, storms have always made me nervous, especially tornado warnings. When the power went off and

Crystal started pacing inside my walk-in closet, I prayed that the storm would pass and there would be no damage. Kevin texted me throughout the tornado so I wouldn't feel scared. The strongest part of the storm lasted for under a minute.

When I reviewed my security camera footage later, I saw the winds blowing on my home—until the screen went black. It turned out that the tornado's path was just a half-mile away. I was grateful there was no exterior damage to my home. There was some damage in the area, and many homes, including mine, had no power. But the temperatures were mild for early December, and that night I slept at home. The next morning, however, the power wasn't back on, and the temperature had dropped. I knew I couldn't stay in my home overnight again, as it would be below freezing. After packing up, Crystal and I stayed with a childhood friend, Jenna, who is now my realtor.

Jenna is a blessing. She helped me find and purchase my townhouse. She sold Mama's property, and during that whole process, I had COVID-19. I couldn't clean out what remained in Mama's home because I was so sick. Jenna took care of purging what remained. She's always there for me—and she went above and beyond what realtors typically do.

After the storm, I had to replace refrigerator items I'd lost after the power outage. Luckily, on Mondays, I pick up healthy meals from a lady who prepares them at a local church, so I wasn't without food. I learned that the Red Cross had set up phones at the church to assist people who were affected by the storm. I wasn't sure how many homes had sustained damage, but I wanted to help others in need. I went to the church and asked, "Is there anyone needing help? My home didn't sustain damage, but others have, and I want to offer someone a room to stay or a place to do laundry, if they need it."

Someone said, "There's a church counselor who might know someone in need."

When I spoke to the counselor on the phone, she wasn't aware of anyone displaced. As we talked, I shared that I'd grown up in an abusive home, and while I hadn't suffered physical abuse, I'm sympathetic to those who do. I told the counselor, "I want to make my home available for anyone in a difficult domestic situation who needs a place to stay. They won't have to pay anything."

I had never considered doing this before, but felt guided to do what I could do to help others. The counselor was receptive to what I offered. She took my name and phone number and said, "I know someone who is in a domestic situation."

A few days later, a woman named Sloan arrived at my home. She was a kind, lovely lady in her mid-forties with beautiful pale skin, blue eyes, and dark hair. Seeing how apprehensive and broken she was, I tried to put her at ease. We talked for a while and were comfortable with each other. Married for over twenty years, Sloan was unhappy. After she told me the circumstances of her imploding marriage, I wanted her to be safe. I offered to let her stay at my home in whatever way she needed.

Sloan couldn't believe I was offering her a place for the days she needed. There were no strings attached to my offer. I explained that when I went through my divorce and stayed with friends, I sometimes had only a couch to sleep on. I told her she was welcome. Over the weeks that followed, she stayed with me more at some times than at others. We got along great, and she was the perfect roommate. It eased my loneliness.

Christmas

Soon, the Christmas season was upon us. I baked and prepared a variety of cookies and other treats for my neighbors. The baking took several hours, and I made accompanying Christmas postcards, which included the names of the treats, a cautionary note of potential peanut allergies, and a note that said, "Merry Christmas from your neighbor." I didn't want Jeff to recognize my name. After 10:00 p.m., I left the prepared bags on each doorstep so no one saw me. Jeff wasn't home, and the next day, it rained. I didn't see his vehicle during this time, so when the bag was gone, I assumed someone had taken it off his porch.

When Kevin asked what I wanted for Christmas, I said, "Only your time." I was hopeful. Although he'd worked long hours close to Christmas, he attended a work Christmas party with me, but he seemed nervous or tired.

I chose gifts for him and his kids. I've not always been the best gift giver, but I wanted to give them meaningful things. I learned how to make a no-sew, hand-tied fleece quilt. No, it wasn't perfect (I'm not Betty Homemaker), but I made Kevin a University of Tennessee orange-and-grey quilt. I pulled special family pictures from his Facebook page and created a photograph calendar, and had an insulated landscaping coffee tumbler made with his company logo on it. I created a Spotify playlist for him with songs that told our story (breakup and all).

Kevin and I made plans for Christmas Eve dinner at his place with Jeremy. David would be with Jane's family. I prepared a turkey dinner and took it over. After dinner, we opened gifts. Kevin and Jeremy loved my personalized gifts. Receiving gifts makes me uncomfortable, as I'd rather give than receive. Kevin gave me a lovely brown wooden tabletop jewelry box, and I looked forward to using the massage gift card he gave me. Then, I opened a thought-provoking card game called *Let's Get Deep*, designed for couples. Because Jeremy was sitting to my left, I was unsure of what to say. *I hope Kevin's ready for real intimacy with me.* Outside, on his porch, Kevin and I asked each other a few questions and gave our innermost answers—it helped us get to know each other better.

I can't wait to ask more questions.

As our night ended, I was happy I got to spend time with Kevin and Jeremy. I'd given Jeremy a drawing pad and pens, and I saw him working on a sketch. He presented me with a drawing of their golden retriever dog, which was spot on.

Kevin said, "Jeremy likes you, and it's a rarity for him to say that."

It made me smile. Before leaving, we shared what we'd be doing with our families on Christmas Day. Also, I remembered I'd been invited to a New Year's Eve gathering with a spiritual group.

New Year's Eve with Our Lady's Group

I've belonged to a small spiritual ladies' group for several years. We share group texts about spiritual thoughts and concerns. A mutual spiritual friend I met ten years ago invited me to a gathering at Alana's marital home out in the country six years ago.

When I first met Alana, she looked familiar. I remembered I'd seen her in Erick's office two years before our affair began. She's been a client of Erick's for several years. Alana and her sister-in-law, Astrid, share similar features, and before I knew them well, I'd call them each other's names. They're both stunning... blonde, beautiful, welcoming, loving, kind, and evolved spiritually.

On New Year's Eve 2023, Alana invited Astrid and me over to meet Jill, a past life regression therapist.

I left town and arrived at Alana's. I drove across a small bridge on her property and experienced the peaceful atmosphere—I heard the birds chirping and a babbling creek and saw deer and squirrels. I felt comfortable there. I didn't want to go back to my place, where it's always hustle and bustle.

Alana has a lovely family home. When these gatherings occur, it's because Astrid and Alana have found others sharing a similar spiritual vision. Both feel they've reincarnated and have shared multiple lives with one another. Our communication is supportive, positive, informational, and uplifting.

Along the way, our spiritual group has talked about many things, including Twin Flames. At one time, I needed an outlet for like-minded people to talk to because I was alone. Alana and Astrid were very familiar with the Twin Flame journey. I protected Erick's identity but gave Alana a copy of my book. She didn't ask who Erick was, but she knew he was a professional. Since we'd known each other for five years and I felt close to her, I said, "I believe you know who my twin is... It's Erick Smith." She smiled. She wasn't shocked. She expressed her love for him and said, "We're all in the same soul family."

As our evening together unfolded, Jill suggested we start the hypnosis sessions, and I was one of her first subjects. Once I was in a hypnotic trance, Jill instructed me to imagine a long hallway with doors on both sides. I was to walk down it, and then stop and open any door. I opened one. I was a crow flying in the sky, and there were many other crows around me. That didn't surprise me, as crows are one of my spirit animals. It's liberating to experience the freedom of flying. I heard cawing. As I parted ways with the other crows, I flew by an upstairs window of a castle and saw a queen inside. After that, I returned to the hallway.

Opening another door and stepping inside, I found myself in a dark area that appeared to be on a ship. Yet I was part of the ship. There were red lights blinking. I didn't like it there—it felt cold and uninviting. I went back to the hallway.

The last door I opened took me into a dazzling white space. *I felt safe.* There was a long, rectangular wooden table, and I sat in a chair on one side of it. Across from me was what I can only describe as a beautiful, white stone pillar of a seated Greek goddess, who moved. I was a little girl, or she was very tall—I had to tilt my head to admire her. Either way, I felt loved and protected. This goddess was my higher self. She didn't speak. When I sensed it was time to leave, I saw three other white stone pillar gods/goddesses moving—but all three were conjoined side-by-side. One was a woman, and two were men. Somehow I felt the woman was me. The men had beards and felt familiar. *Is one of them Erick's higher self?*

Coming out of hypnosis, I was emotional. "If what I saw has anything to do with the afterlife," I told the ladies, "I can't wait to be there, because it was peaceful." I allowed what I saw to sink in. In the future, I hope to have another session with Jill.

Spiritualists

My spiritual quest of consulting hypnotists, spiritual readers, mediums, and other practitioners' services, in order to remember and realize my purpose, will continue. The information I receive helps me with my personal growth.

Readers and mediums have told me that Erick's higher self and mine are focused more on me and my growth because he's stubborn and isn't doing his work according to his soul contract. So, the hell he's been through will continue.

If I could tell him anything, it would be, "Quit being stubborn. Move out of your own way. Get out of ego and pride. Don't ignore your intuition. Go within and listen to your higher self. It's not too late to make better decisions. You're destined to repeat the same lessons, karma, and hell again next lifetime if you don't do your soul healing work while here on earth." I pray Erick's lower vibration doesn't affect my higher energy. Because we mirror one another, it could. I hope my vibration helps him when things are difficult for him, without him taking my energy.

A week passed, and Jill texted me. As a channeler, she sometimes receives messages for people, and she'd received one for me. "I'm being told for you to pay careful attention to the part where you see yours and Erick's souls together. There's a message for healing and self-love in it because something isn't how you previously thought it was."

Two weeks later, I texted Jill. "What you referred to when you sent me your message happened last night. I saw my twin and my soul together through my third eye, and then I saw something else. Erick and I dissipated, and I saw what looked similar to a dark alien."

What did this mean? Why would we disappear and an alien be what was revealed? Later, Alana and I spoke. She'd microdosed mushrooms the night before, so she was still connected. She thinks Erick and I are together in other realities. "You were both interdimensional beings before you came here, although you didn't see that." She felt that Erick and I are amongst the oldest of souls.

Interdimensional beings are entities or beings that are thought to travel between different dimensions of time and space. What I saw through my third eye didn't look like the aliens that I've seen in science fiction movies. It was different. There's still a lot for me to learn.

Chapter Twenty

Stepping Away

The Homeowners' Association of our neighborhood complex notified us of an upcoming meeting at their office. They were going to increase our monthly dues by $90. This was one meeting I couldn't miss. On the night of the meeting, Jeff left his home at the same time I was pulling out of my driveway.

I sat in the business parking lot, trying to soothe my nerves. I mustered up the courage to go inside the meeting room. Jeff sat on one side of the room, and I was on the opposite side. As I mentioned, Jeff and Erick look alike—there's no mistaking they're brothers. I felt anxious—my face was flushed. There were angry homeowners in the room, especially some women, whom I sensed were in their masculine energy. When I asked a question, I sensed Jeff looking at me.

As soon as the meeting was over, I bolted. My intuition is strong, but with my anxiousness, I felt my perception was less. *If he knows who I am, does he judge me?* My Tarot cards and pendulum revealed that, "Yes, he knows who I am—the woman his brother had an affair with."

As I mentioned earlier, once I knew who Jeff was, I was on edge in the complex. Whenever Crystal and I walked by his place on our way home from the bark park, I looked straight ahead—never toward his place. One day, at the end of January, I was walking to the community mailbox, and out of the corner of my eye, I saw Jeff in his truck. He pulled out of his driveway, let his window down, and smiled at me.

OMG, they look exactly alike.

"Thanks for the Christmas candy," he said.

How did he know it was me? I didn't sign the card.

"You're welcome. But I'm not a good cook."

"You're a phenomenal baker," he said. "I'm Jeff."

I know who you are. He sounds similar to Erick. Charming... just like Erick. "I'm V.C."

We parted ways.

I saw Erick's truck at Jeff's place three times. One day, while walking Crystal, I saw Erick's truck in Jeff's driveway. I stopped at my mailbox, which was across from Jeff's place. *Did Erick see me?* Another day, I was walking Crystal and saw Erick's truck on our street. I'm not sure if he saw me, but I looked in his direction. It's ironic—my security camera (that Erick had paid for) footage showed him at Jeff's. To my knowledge, Karen wasn't with him any of those times, but Erick's truck had tinted windows, so I couldn't see if she was ever with him.

Two weeks after Jeff complimented me on my baking skills, he moved out of his townhouse. In recent weeks, there had been a lady at his place. I think he moved in with her. I was relieved. I could breathe.

Mirroring Twin Flame

Texting Kevin, I told him I wanted to try something I've done with two other people—a friend and Larry. "A bond can be unbreakable if you look into each other's eyes for two minutes," I told him. "I want to try this with you—just lie down together, and be in the moment. Just be."

He asked, "I assume you want me to sleep with you?"

That annoyed me. "No, that isn't what I mean." I elaborated, saying:

This feels different. I want to be in your energy, but I wonder if you want me too—sometimes I don't think you do. This has been hard. Attraction naturally includes intimacy in relationships, and without it, things stay in the friendship zone. I could have focused on rejection, but I've chosen not to go down that path.

"Don't think that. That's not the case. It's complicated," he said.

Feeling a trigger starting, I needed him to say something to keep me from going deep inside my mind. "Tell me something that's inside your heart and mind... something a woman should hear." *It shouldn't be this complicated.*

Kevin texted back:

All my life, the only thing I've ever wanted is true, unconditional love. Too often, I rushed into things instead of letting them play out. This ruined any chance of true love ever developing. When I met you, I knew I'd found something special. You're everything a guy looks for in a woman... beautiful, intelligent, and kind-hearted. I want to do this right. I want this to last. How a relationship develops in the early stages sets the tone for what it will become later in life. I'm not in this for instant gratification. I'm in this hoping to set the tone for something beautiful that will last a lifetime.

My heart was overcome with love. "These are the most special words anyone ever said to me. I want all that, too." Kevin had helped me to lessen my triggers and not internalize situations. I texted:

> *When Twin Flames trigger you, it creates growth through lessons. I've tried to determine if you're a soulmate or something deeper. You feel familiar and comforting—if not a soulmate, then what? With God taking my pain, this feels like a Divine connection. As a twin, I'm learning lessons from my soul contract. My abandonment and rejection wounds get triggered when I don't see you because I love you and want closeness. I ask myself: "Why am I triggered? What is this teaching me?" I'm having the full Twin Flame experience with you—this is what's supposed to happen.*

The healing that should've been what happened with Erick... Could Kevin be a mirroring Twin Flame for me?

Mirroring twins enter our lives when we're separated from our Twin Flames. They serve as a catalyst of growth and reflect similar wounding and patterns, and reveal areas we still need to work on. It's an intense connection and can feel familiar, just as it does with a Twin Flame.

It's the only explanation... Kevin's a mirroring Twin Flame.

Winter Bleakness

Close to the end of January, the snow and ice were gone. Kevin and I had seen each other last at dinner three weeks ago and once when I'd dropped by his home for a few minutes. Kevin hadn't texted me on Saturday, but since I knew he was behind in his work since we saw a lot of snow earlier in the month, I assumed he worked that day and was catching up. In the late afternoon, I texted, "Are you working?"

"No," he said. "I've been painting and playing with the kids."

I felt disappointed and triggered. *He'll never make me a priority, and I need to accept it.* I texted:

I can't keep doing this. You're full of intent but lack action. You say you think of me but don't reach out. I avoid texting when you're working and behind in your work. You don't answer my game questions. Your answers satisfy me briefly, but we haven't spent time together this winter despite you saying you want to.

You've dangled a carrot in front of my nose. I'm tired of breadcrumbs. If you want to be with me, I need more action. If you can't make this a full relationship, tell me. What's between us is special—I don't want to lose it. Is this how you've treated past relationships? You said we needed more effort—I've been willing, but you haven't. You said you'd put me ahead of your needs, but that hasn't happened.

This could be beautiful between us. I've been understanding and patient, but I can't continue like this, Kevin.

Kevin understood. He wrote:

My life is a series of things I must do. I work, and if it rains on weekends, I need that time with my kids—especially David, who I only have three days a week. I've dealt with this complaint in every relationship, even when married. I don't know how to make time for myself. When I'm not working, I'm sleeping or doing house maintenance.

I'm a business owner and single dad—free time is rare. My divorce made this worse. I now handle everything alone, plus care for two children, one with a terminal illness. I may not be able to give you the time and attention you need right now. I don't want it to be that way, but it's what it is.

That was the truthful answer I didn't want to see. I texted back: "I don't want us to be apart, but that's discounting my wants and needs. For now, it's best that we step away from each other. I love you."

He replied, "In that case, I wish you the best."

Tears filled my eyes. I was completing a University of Tennessee no-sew fleece blanket for Wendy's birthday, so I focused on that, trying to avoid facing the fact that it was over. I finished David's Tennessee Titans blanket earlier in the week for his birthday. Late that night, I finished the blanket. I gathered Wendy's and David's blankets and drove to Kevin's home to leave them on the front porch.

Valentine's Day was two weeks away, and I'd already picked out a perfect card and ordered a personalized gift the week before, and they'd already arrived in my mail. The gift was a placard with our likeness and names. We were sitting, coffees in hand, in Adirondack chairs on the front porch. When I saw the inscription, "God gave me you," I knew it was the right gift to order. It captured what my heart felt in those four words.

During my drive, I knew I'd be quiet and not wake anyone. I left a note: "You have and will continue to affect my life. I'd hoped for you to fight for us. Know that I'll always love you unconditionally. Always, V.C."

Chapter Twenty-One

Yearning and Burning

Kevin isn't the first man who's changed me, but he's the one who brought out the best in me, and in my relationship with him, I experienced constant healing and ultimate improvement, despite being triggered. He marked my soul. The long, wintry days reflected my sad, broken heart. Breakups are worse when intimacy has been part of the equation.

In a week's time, I was traveling to meet my grandchildren, so I found a thread of happiness during the sad time following our breakup.

Beth had developed pre-eclampsia at thirty-three weeks, and the twins, Lilli and Reese, were delivered by Cesarean section at thirty-four weeks the morning after Christmas. Twelve days later, they were both at home. I delayed my visit until they were six weeks old.

Everyone says the love you feel toward grandchildren differs from what you feel with your own children. I was excited to meet the twins. When I first held Lilli and Reese, joy filled my heart, and the photo Roman took revealed my huge smile and a new happiness. They were tiny, but healthy. Lilli is the big sister, with dark hair. Reese was bald. Reese reminded me of Roman, while Lilli resembled Beth. I was rusty at taking care of a baby, much less two, but I loved holding and cuddling them. I wished Mama could've held them. Lilli is angelic, and Reese is determined. She'll be gentle, and he'll speak up when needed.

While I was visiting, Kevin texted me: "I've enjoyed seeing your Facebook posts with your grandbabies. I hope you're doing well."

We exchanged a few friendly texts.

I asked, "Do you still think about me?"

"Of course I think about you."

"I can't get you off my mind. I miss you so much. You're in my dreams."

My hopes were dashed when he replied, "You said it yourself, and it's true. I don't have time to devote to a relationship right now. Free time is something I never have."

I said, "I wanted to ask."

"Hopefully one day the stars will align."

"I hope sooner than later. Just know you've changed me in many positive ways. You helped me see my worth. I have a sense of gratitude for that. My love for you will remain."

Three weeks passed.

One day, clairaudiently, I heard Kevin's stargaze text tone, so I felt he would reach out. Then, out of the blue, that familiar text tone alerted me. We texted and caught up. It saddened me to learn that after a long battle with alcoholism, his uncle had passed.

Knowing how hard it can be to go through the motions of a funeral and that he would be a pallbearer, I hesitated, but the next day, I reached out. Although I didn't know his uncle and even though we'd broken up, I wanted to be a support to Kevin and his family to hold space for their grief. I asked if he would be okay with me coming to the visitation, and he was.

Having never met his large Catholic family, I was nervous, especially knowing I'd meet Wendy. It was a cold, dreary winter day. When I arrived at the funeral home, Kevin was outside smoking. He looked handsome in his suit. We hugged. Upon entering, he introduced me to his family.

Kevin's family was warm and kind to me. The memorial video revealed Kevin's strong resemblance to his uncle. Wendy is a beautiful woman in her seventies. I felt the love between mother and son. During the visitation, we watched the funeral video—it was full of photos, and I felt honored to see events from Kevin's childhood.

I asked, "Do you want me to attend the Catholic Mass?

"I don't want you to feel obligated, but you can if you want to."

Kevin and I drove in my car to the country church, the oldest Catholic church in continuous operation in our state. Having never attended a Catholic funeral, I saw the pomp and circumstance of tradition. They laid his uncle to rest in the frigid temperatures. Kevin stood next to me for the last words and prayer. We left in my vehicle and stopped at a gas station. Upon coming out, Kevin had purchased a red rose, which he gave to me, saying, "A pretty rose for a pretty lady."

Following the service, Kevin's family planned to go to his grandparents' home to have pizza. He invited me to go with him. It's a childhood home he'd spent time at, and he had wonderful memories of it. Wendy and I had a good rapport. His youngest aunt was funny!

Kevin said he appreciated me coming. He asked me to go out for dinner with him in the coming days, and I told him I would. We ended the evening outside with a hug. Our texting started again. We'd missed each other. Revealing that the images I see through my third eye had increased, I told Kevin I had seen us together, in "detailed movie clips." He wasn't sure what it meant when I told him that the images weren't from this lifetime.

We met at a buffet for dinner. Kevin dropped David off at Jane's. It was great to see him again. After dinner, we sat in my car and talked for a while. I had a list of things I needed to say. I told him I'd wanted consistency, for him to integrate me into his life. I hadn't wanted to be a convenient option. "You're guarded when touch and intimacy are involved. You don't let me in."

He listened, but promised nothing.

Before I left, when I asked if we were ready to announce on Facebook that we were "in a relationship."

"Sure!" he said.

Within a few days, it had been a year since he'd found me on the dating app. He wished me a "Happy Facebook" anniversary.

Our next date was at the park where our first date had ended. Kevin wanted to have a picnic with me. Jane kept David. It was a romantic gesture. I'd never been on a picnic (other than at the same place when I was on a field trip in sixth grade with classmates). We saw many couples dressed in high-school prom-style clothing. It was a beautiful evening, though cool. Kevin had made us sandwiches wrapped in aluminum foil and had chips for us. He was relaxed with me.

When it got cold, he wanted us to sit in my car, so we did. I smiled and said, "I have a gift for you."

For my fiftieth birthday, I'd gifted myself with a boudoir photo session, as I'd wanted to capture myself in sexy photos before I aged. Most women need a drink to relax when having a boudoir session, but not me. I was a natural at the session and felt empowered. They applied professional makeup and styled my hair. Although the photographer had lingerie available, I'd brought along my personal favorites. I encourage every woman to do a photo shoot. Men, buy your significant other this gift. Trust me, it will be one of your favorite gifts.

Part of the boudoir session was a View-Master with select photos. I'd kept it to give to a man who was special, but no relationship had stood the test of time. Despite my confidence, the photos were of me forty pounds heavier and with short red hair in an inverted-bob style. Before we parted ways that night, I took Kevin's hand in mine and kissed it. I said I had something for him and gave him the View-Master, although I felt apprehensive because of my previous size. I asked him to open it after I left.

Almost immediately, he texted, "They're beautiful."

I said, "I've been waiting to give them to someone special that I love. You're special, Kevin."

Things were going well, and I was happy. When our next date was delayed, I asked him to make me glad I'd waited to see him. He wanted me to say what, but I told him to surprise me... LOL. (A bit of romantic time.)

"My sex drive has fallen in the last few years," Kevin said. "However, I've gotten my testosterone injection refilled. I've been waiting for the right time to start them again." He said he wanted to make love to me and knew the shot would help him. Kevin asked, "Would you be willing to give me the injection?"

I told him I would. It would be difficult for me to give myself a shot.

Overall, men's and women's libidos decrease as we age. It meant the world to me that he trusted me and had told me. We knew it would most likely be awkward, as we hadn't ventured into this area. But he was ready.

"I've tried my best to be patient." He had my heart.

I felt vulnerable and texted, "I want you to make love to me... It's hard for me to say those words. When I see us through my third eye, it isn't only the action, but all things. However, I worry about how I'll be after radiation and menopause." It had been over fifteen months since I'd been intimate with anyone, and these were genuine worries for me, besides him being with younger women than me in his past, plus our four-year age difference. Kevin asked if I wanted to meet for a movie after he got finished with work.

Kevin and I both love reggae and Bob Marley, so on our next date, we saw a movie about Marley's life. The movie was great, and the music spoke to me. Since we weren't going back to his place after our date, we sat in his car in the movie theater parking lot. I knew he'd brought a vial of testosterone with him, because he was working a lot and it would be the right time to start the injections. He asked me again if I would inject it for him after the movie. That seemed like a caring thing to do. He explained the injection process. Since I'd never given an injection, I was nervous—I didn't want to hurt him. Once it was drawn up, he dropped his jeans.

Nervous, I squeezed his upper right thigh and gave him the injection. He looked toward his car window. The medication is thick, and it took a while for the injection to be complete. Kevin said I did great—he'd barely felt it.

Wanting him to feel my love, I kissed him. Suddenly, he kissed me deeply. I felt the genuine passion he'd been suppressing. Whereas I normally ended up almost on top of him when we made out in the car, he pushed me back against my seat. He'd been holding back... way back!

We were in that sensual moment without awkwardness. I hadn't felt this since Erick and I experienced an all-consuming passion.

He kissed my neck gently. When we pulled apart, my body and thoughts were spinning. I said, "That felt like being a teenager again."

He agreed. I didn't want to leave, but he had an early morning.

When I got out of the car to return to mine, my thoughts were jumbled and my sense of direction was off. I laughed out loud because I was walking in the wrong direction.

Driving on an interstate going home, my body and mind were still in a blissful state. I made a wrong turn. I texted him: "You scattered my brain... and I liked it." My lips were numb and throbbing all at the same time. He had me, mind, body, heart, and soul. I felt a real burning and yearning. The sensual part of my Divine Feminine is strong.

"I think we're two imperfect souls who are perfect together," I texted.

Kevin agreed.

Chapter Twenty-Two

Fighting the Downward Spiral

Easter came, and Kevin invited me to his place to celebrate. It was an enormous step, as I'd be meeting Jane and David. He'd told me not to expect too much of David, and because I have two sons, I understood.

It took all the unconditional love within me to meet Jane. I prayed our meeting would be graceful and warm, and I resolved to be kind when we met.

Kevin's getting the best version of me. In recent days, I feel I can open myself up. I know there's always room for improvement, but with what has transpired along my Twin Flame experience, the healing I've worked for, and my soul purification makes me blessed.

It was a beautiful, warm, sunny day in late March. I wore an aqua tee shirt, white capri pants, and white sandals. When I pulled into Kevin's driveway, Jane walked onto the front porch. *Is she sizing me up or being territorial?* She had extremely long hair, wore no makeup, and had on a long pastel pink and white vertical striped sundress with brownish sandals (similar to Birkenstocks). *I'm not jealous. I don't feel intimidated.*

Extending my hand, I smiled, introduced myself, and said, "It's nice to meet you." She just looked at me. It was as comfortable as I could expect to be around her. I sensed she didn't like my confidence. I walked past her into the house. She followed. I wore a smile continuously. David was as Kevin had described. I tried to talk with him, but he had little to say.

Has Jane said something negative about me?

Kevin, Jane, and I placed Easter eggs around his yard and in the neighbor's empty backyard, and while Wendy's tardiness caused a delay in the Easter egg hunt, because I'm talkative, there wasn't a lack of conversation. We sat on Kevin's front porch. Jane saw the crystals I wore and asked, "Don't they mean different things?"

"Yes," I said. I thought she might ask something else about the crystals, but she didn't.

When Wendy arrived, she brought gifts for the kids. Jane watched Wendy and me interact positively. Not long after, Wendy and the kids hunted for eggs. My contribution was Pokémon cards and prize eggs containing state quarters and older coins with their birth years on them. Wendy and the kids had a lot of fun looking for the prize eggs. At the end, Jeremy had the most eggs in his bag. Kevin and I checked to see if any eggs remained in the neighbor's yard. Back in the house, David had spread all of his eggs, candy, and prizes on the oak hardwood floors. I sat down on the floor beside Jane and helped pick David's winnings up. She seemed irritated at me and didn't thank me for helping. Before I left, Kevin told me that since their divorce, I'd been the first romantic interest either parent had introduced to David, so I knew the importance of setting the future tone for other holidays.

Kevin said he'd appreciated what I'd done for his kids for the Easter celebration.

Later, we resumed the twenty questions game. Kevin asked, "What's the worst mistake you ever made?"

"Having the affair," I said. "But if I hadn't, I wouldn't be who I am... a better person. I wasn't my authentic self and was unhappy. The affair triggered me to see what I was missing in my life. It allowed me to know how I could love (without limitations)."

Our connection was getting stronger. I heard a clairaudient song by an American rap artist, Tone Loc. I'd only channeled songs from Erick and his higher self before. Now, I felt I'd picked up on a song Kevin had been thinking of at the same time. So I asked Kevin, "Do you like Tone Loc?"

"I do," he said.

I asked, "Was my intuition accurate?"

"Well, certainly."

We made plans for the weekend, but COVID-19 took over his household again. As I mentioned earlier, since downsizing my business, I had more free time than Kevin did. I offered to do some administrative work to help him out, but he declined.

"Everything I write is in 'Kevin code,'" he said. "It only makes sense to me."

Since he didn't need my help, I had downtime, so I planned to attend a highly anticipated solar eclipse three hours away.

The Solar Eclipse

Three months before my fall onto the bathroom tile, in August 2017, there'd been a total solar eclipse. I'd been fortunate to witness it within a mile of the centerline of the eclipse's path. Eclipse energies are powerful. I believe those energies changed my life and contributed to my spiritual awakening.

Almost seven years later, knowing a second, longer solar eclipse was coming, I felt drawn to attend. I traveled to the Angel Mounds near Evansville, Indiana, to watch it with my friend, Summer. I sensed there would be bookend energy and was excited to see what would happen. *How will this eclipse affect me? After what transpired with the first one* (my physical fall, spiritual awakening, affair, and divorce)*, will this cause a negative outcome with Kevin?* That thought was in the back of my mind.

When the eclipse started, the atmosphere was like the first eclipse. The sky had a green hue, which put me in mind of tornado warnings. At the moment of totality, I wore my protective solar eclipse glasses. I saw what looked like the logo of a horror movie, *The Ring*, which freaked me out some. However, it was amazing to experience. *Powerful energy.* The totality was over in three minutes—longer than the 2017 eclipse.

When the eclipse ended, I said goodbye to Summer and drove home. Close to Angel Mounds, I passed a church. Surprisingly, I saw five nuns walking outside in only their underskirts, without the black overlay. That felt odd.

Alana told me she'd felt I'd had a connection with Catholicism—and that perhaps I'd been a nun in a previous life. I know little about Catholicism but have several connections to it since my divorce. In seven years, I've been involved with five men affiliated with the Catholic faith: Luke, the ex-priest; Kevin, a former altar boy and cradle Catholic; Erick, also a cradle Catholic; Jim, a former altar boy and cradle Catholic; and Jake (twelve years younger than me and attended a Catholic school Luke had taught at). This boggles my mind. Am I experiencing karma from another life? During my Ayahuasca journeys, I've seen Catholic symbolism and clerical clothing, so I know it's more than coincidence.

I've tried using my spiritual gifts to understand what my Catholic connection is. My intuition arrives when I least expect it, but it hasn't given me those answers. It started niggling at me again about Kevin, and to keep my anxiety in check, I reached out to him via text.

You have me in all ways. You let me love you and seem to accept it. I want our love to grow. If you have doubts about your feelings, promise not to hide them or spare mine.

I prayed to handle meeting Jane with kindness, grace, and unconditional love, which I did. I also know if you want to be with her, there's nothing I can do. We all have free will. You say there's friendship, but those were the same words you used in October before saying you still loved her.

My intuition has been bothering me since Monday, leading me to lay my cards out. A trusted reader confirmed what mine showed—Jane may approach you if she hasn't already. The cards show possible jealousy toward me. I admire how you both put David first. But if she approaches you, it's about security, not love. Intuitively, I feel she tries to maintain control over you.

Kevin reassured me there was nothing between Jane and him, other than David. When he'd thought he wanted to be with her again, he'd forgotten all the reasons it didn't work the first time. They got along better as friends, no feelings involved. He reassured me and my anxiety when he said, "Please don't worry about things like this. You have my heart."

Relief overcame me. He eased my mind.

I told Kevin:

When you came into my life, I let you in but held back parts of myself I didn't think anyone could have. Others who've done spiritual work like me were "rewarded" by Divine—our hard work didn't go unnoticed. You were brought into my life as my result. I prayed for God to bring you and to release my pain. But when you entered, neither of us was ready. We're ready now.

Kevin told me he didn't believe in "twins" but supported my beliefs. I told him it's okay for us to not have the same beliefs, as I knew it was hard for most people to comprehend my truth. If I hadn't experienced all that I have, I most likely wouldn't believe it either.

I know that so much of my healing has been unfolding through my relationship with Kevin. However, this life journey is about loving yourself and healing wounds. Elohee is where my real healing began, and I was expecting to return soon.

The Turning Point

My next trip to Elohee was almost here. It had been two weeks since I'd seen Kevin—to drop off a casserole—when David tested positive for COVID-19 again. When I asked if we were going to see each other before I left, Kevin said he wanted to, but his day was full and he'd have David until the evening. My rejection wounding came up. I asked him to make time for me, but I knew he didn't have it.

"David is only here six more weeks, and then he'll be with Jane, out-of-state for six weeks."

I asked him to come and stay with me after my return from Elohee. "We don't have to have sex, although I want to."

Kevin couldn't come over, because he gets up early for work. He wanted to just schedule a date when I returned from Elohee.

The next words in my text to him changed our trajectory.

"Why don't you come by after work on Thursday when I return? Kevin, I want to make love, I want to fuck. I want to feel all parts of you."

Four hours went by without a response. Inside, I felt devastation and a trigger coming. I needed a response.

"I don't know what you want me to say to 'I want to fuck.'"

Never have I ever wanted to take back my words more.

"That isn't all I want. You know that. I love you in all ways. When you and I were together in the car, and you let yourself go, all parts of me came alive. I hoped you wanted me in all ways. There's such chemistry. I didn't mean to offend you. Sometimes I'm blunt. Can you forgive me?"

Although Kevin said he wants so much more than that and I didn't have to apologize, I knew I'd messed up. It hurt me to know I was on the delivery side of a trigger-inflicting wound. I was beside myself.

He revealed that in his marriage, Jane had expressed similar thoughts.

"I'm sorry. I don't want to be anything like her. I had a moment of weakness because I want to be with you."

He didn't respond for several hours. My anxiety was horrible. I couldn't take it and asked, "Are we okay?"

When he said, "As far as I know…?" I was relieved. But my anxiety stayed with me as my constant companion. My intuition bothered me after I left home for the drive to Elohee.

Elohee Revisited

My drive to Elohee in early spring is always a mix of many shades of spring greens and winter blandness. There are many twists and turns on the drive. But whenever I reach Hogpen Gap, I know my peace is within reach.

Before arriving at Elohee, I drove through Helen, Georgia, to see the Nacoochee Indian Mound. It was at the center of the ancient Cherokee town of Gauxule, and according to legend, in his search for gold, Spanish explorer Hernando de Soto visited there in 1540. The mound is 150 feet wide and 20 feet high. The Cherokee people performed ceremonial dances in and around the Town House—but that's long gone.

I imagined the ancestors of my Cherokee Grandpa living their best lives and joining with other tribe members, performing ceremonial dances in traditional headdresses, breechcloths, dresses, and moccasins around the mound. I felt connected, like I was a part of something bigger. I had a sense of belonging to something that transcends time and space. After leaving, I made the short drive to Elohee. I thought about the idea of belonging and knew that I wanted to see Kevin when I got home to talk about our future.

The flowers at Elohee were in bloom, and the purple, yellow, and white irises were among my favorites. Elohee is my second home. Healing improvements always happen while I'm there. It makes sense. I love the land because the Cherokee people lived on the mountain. I have only a small percentage of Native American in my bloodline, but I feel connected to my heritage. Like many Cherokee people, I have a straight nose and high cheekbones, but my skin tone is pale. When I die, I plan to be cremated, and I asked the administrators of Elohee if a part of my ashes could be placed by the waterfall. They agreed.

While at Elohee, I normally attend activities unless I'm sick with upper respiratory issues. The allergens differ from where I live. On that trip, I suffered with a sinus headache and didn't feel well, so I stayed to myself. As I've shared, I've attended seven Elohee retreats in the past three years, and there's nothing I enjoy more. It enriches my soul's growth each time. Retreats at Elohee give me emotional healing I haven't been able to replicate.

This time, I knew that for me to move forward with Kevin, I needed to use my time at Elohee to do more purging and releasing my Twin Flame attachment to Erick. The preoccupation with our twin is difficult—it's like trying to pull yourself out of quicksand.

This gathering was the largest group of ladies to be at a retreat since I started attending "Dragonfly" retreats at Elohee three years ago. After dinner, eighteen ladies made their way to Forest Studio for Connecting and Opening the Circle. As I do when I attend any spiritual event, I carried my vintage sarong Divine Feminine quilt with me. I wrapped myself in it while sitting on a yoga chair. We opened the windows and let the cool spring night breeze flow through the space.

It was interesting to watch the mix of energy with old friends and new acquaintances. The group has unfamiliar faces, but in some way, the same players. When I walked in, I felt drawn to the energy of a lovely young lady. I sat on my yoga chair with the thin mat underneath. Looking at her, I smiled and said, "Your energy is beautiful!" Her name tag read "Shannon."

Shannon looked at me and asked, "Did you write a book?"

"Yes."

"Is it about Twin Flames?"

"Yes." *How did she know?*

Then she said, "I read it twice. It inspired and helped me."

That was the definitive sign I'd asked God for… finishing my manuscript. I asked her how she'd known it was me.

"I saw your name tag."

When Shannon said she'd come to the Dragonfly retreat because she'd read my book, I was humbled. With my first book, I'd hoped to make a difference in people's lives, and it had done that for her. I'm still in awe that she'd traveled six hundred miles to attend Elohee because she'd read my words.

Knowing I'd inspired Shannon allowed me to not remain stagnant in completing my next manuscript. I opened my draft on my laptop and resumed writing. However, still under the weather from the allergens, I stayed in bed part of the time, too.

My time at Elohee was spinning by. On Wednesday, I texted Kevin. "Can you come over after I get home?" No response. Then, when he texted back, I fell apart.

"I can't because I work Friday," he wrote. "Can I be honest? I'm not, and will never be, interested in scheduling a 'screw' date. For me, it has to happen over the course of an actual date. I need it to be spontaneous. I don't care about the idea of, 'We're gonna have sex on Thursday at 9:00 p.m.' That's not romantic to me."

He didn't know that I'd felt a need to schedule our time together because his time was limited and he didn't stay with me after dates. *I feel disgusted with myself.*

I was spiraling out of control. "That isn't what it was going to be."

Kevin replied, "Wasn't it, though?"

"I texted you what I can't take back. Elohee heals me. That's why I wanted you to come over. I wanted to connect, for you to see me after an Elohee retreat—to see me in a pure form. I said I was sorry. I just wanted to spend time together. That type of 'date' isn't for me either. I was trying to offer a time that wouldn't interfere with the time you spend with David. Kevin, I'm loving and kind. This hurts."

Then he said, "I'm basing this off of the past several times you've asked me to come to your house."

Adrenaline pumped through my body. I was angry, hurt, and confused. Elohee wouldn't help me this time. The hurt was too much. By texting those four words I couldn't take back, I'd brought the house of cards down. I didn't know how to fix it or save myself from the downward spiral.

"You haven't been to my house in over four months," I texted. "I thought you wanted to spend time with me. You said you wanted to make love to me."

"I know what I said."

"Kevin, I see so many things with you. I triggered you, and I felt terrible about it. I've never scheduled that with anyone I've been in a relationship with. It comes organically for me."

My anxious attachment style reared its ugly head for the rest of the retreat. I deferred the group nature walk, stayed in my room, and laid Tarot cards to get insight. Fear took over. It was over between us. Because I suffer from abandonment and rejection in relationships, my thought process leads to illogical thoughts. Every wound rises to the surface and leads to triggers.

I created this. That pained me.

After eating lunch, I went for a much-needed massage. It was a cool, sunny spring day. I put on a light jacket and went to the meditation rocks and sat, allowing myself to think deep thoughts. A short while later, I followed the red heart trail to my favorite spot, the waterfall. I've seen its water cascading down; however, this time, because of decreased rainfall, the waterfall was smaller. For an hour, I was alone, and I lay on the hammock and listened to the calming water. There's a small black bench to the right of the waterfall, and I sat on it for a while. Then, the other ladies started to arrive, and I realized they had received some kind of advance instructions about what to do there. *What am I missing?*

Be brave, I told myself. *Be strong. Don't cry.* My clan—the ladies I often met at the retreat—sat in silence. I was still sitting on a bench, and my empathic friend, Emily, whom I'd met three years before at my first retreat, came and sat beside me. She put her arm around me, and I teared up. I fought to keep my tears to myself. Internally, I was sobbing.

I knew Emily felt my sad energy. She's one of the most compassionate, beautiful, and loving women I've ever known. Emily knew what I needed at that moment. She gave me a loving hug and held me.

Realizing I'd messed up, I knew I wouldn't text Kevin. I felt terrible for the pain I'd caused him. Eight hours later, he texted and apologized for his attitude that morning. He'd found out he had to buy a new $15,000 mower for his business. I'd texted him just when he'd heard that news.

"I'm sorry," he said.

I was sorry for the enormous expense he'd had. I texted:

It felt like you saw me as a slut. At the waterfall, I released that pain. Kevin, I love you. I'm sexual and sensual, but when I say I want to be held, it's not about sex—sometimes I just miss human connection.

I express love through touch and don't want guilt about this part of me. As Divine Feminine, sexuality and sensuality are huge parts of who I am. Though I have wants and needs, I know how wounded you are. I wish I could take my text back. I want us to move forward without sadness or anger. Romance is something I want and need—it's a huge part of love for me.

He texted:

Believe me, romance is huge for me too. I'm still deep in healing and, for maybe the first time, I'm not always sure what to do next. I know I'm a better person than I've been in a long time. Being vulnerable is hard because it requires trust I'm not sure I have. I'm not saying I don't trust you specifically—I have a hard time trusting women's intentions. It's going to take time.

Kevin's therapist had moved, so he was no longer in therapy. I texted:

Vulnerability leads to healing. Healing leads to trust. Please trust me. With all I've gone through, I shouldn't trust you, but I do. I hope you'll find a therapist who can help you. Meet me in the middle. Take a chance and let your heart open to me. I want it in all ways, but you must allow it. I could've chosen not to trust men's intentions—I have every right. But part of why I'm here is to love people. Divine gave me that gift, and I hope you'll receive and reciprocate it. Someone once said they didn't understand how I remain open to love after how I've been treated. I never want to be hardened. I'm still working on forgiving myself. You've triggered me at times, leading to further healing and allowing me to give you my heart.

Knowing he didn't believe spiritually as I do, and leans toward traditionalism, I asked him to consider allowing me to do two things besides my morning prayer. I wanted to offer a Reiki clearing, which would involve clearing his chakras, and asked if he would let me. "You won't 'feel' anything," I said, "but if it works, it might help you. Sound healing would also be beneficial, as the frequencies would help."

Since Kevin wasn't sure what any of that was, I knew he was skeptical. He supported me believing in whatever I wanted to, but my beliefs couldn't differ from his.

He wasn't sure he was open to this.

After I arrived home from Elohee, Kevin's texts were generalized and without depth, and of course my intuition niggled at me. It felt like a shoe was going to drop.

I hate this.

Kevin hadn't texted me in two days. Two weeks after Elohee, I was on Facebook and reviewed my personal information, and saw my relationship status with him wasn't the same, so I looked at his profile. When I saw "single," my heart dropped. I thought I might vomit. Upset, I called him, but he didn't answer. So, I left a voice message, "When did you decide you were single? You should've told me."

I couldn't believe his next words. "You can't seriously call what we're doing 'a relationship.' You know I don't have time for a relationship. We've both known that for a year. You're a great person. You'll make someone a great wife. I don't have the time to devote to another person. My plate as a single dad/ business owner is full."

"I can't believe you didn't have the courtesy to tell me. I never expected that from you, of all people. I thought you loved me."

"I'm sorry," he said. "I just worked a fourteen-hour day. I'm exhausted and can't do this right now. I'll reach out tomorrow."

Confusion, hurt, and anger set in. Many thoughts kept me awake that night.

The next day, Kevin texted:

I'm sorry. My schedule can't accommodate a relationship right now. At least one that's fair to you. You deserve so much more than I can give you. I struggle to make time for my kids right now. I know you'll find the right person who can devote the time and effort you deserve. I'm sorry it's not me. I must grind for the next few years to retire and enjoy life as I'm supposed to. I don't see things slowing soon. Please believe me when I say that I wish you all the best that life offers. I hope we can remain friends. Kevin.

His response was sterile. This wasn't fair. I'd overlooked the warning signs, but I'd been hoping the situation would settle. I'm sick of men telling me what I deserve, when they're saying it so they don't feel guilty when discarding me. Sadly, I wanted to inflict daggers:

You're being casual, like you're doing me a favor. I'm angry. You handled this in a cowardly way—you're emotionally unavailable.

How can you dispose of me like I don't matter? You can't be in a healthy, loving relationship. You should've told me you wouldn't invest in me, not let me find out coldly. You said you wanted more with me. Why didn't you tell me instead of letting me discover it this way? I thought you loved and cared for me. I've had more patience than most.

I gave you space and time, but you breadcrumb me and don't share. Selfish. I've only been kind, loving, and compassionate. This is you, not me. You don't know how to open your heart and accept love. Intimacy is part of relationships, and I've lost a year sexually, believing you wanted that too.

Just because I expressed my physical wants, his rejection made me feel guilty about this part of myself. That was a tough pill to swallow. My needs didn't matter to him. It's unfair. If he went on another dating app, I told him, I hoped he didn't mess someone else up, like he had me. Fully in ego, words in my mind screamed and escaped my lips. *Screw you, Kevin.*

After that text exchange, I had a split-second choice to make. Either I'd continue repeating my trigger pattern of going into the pit of emotional hell or fight and not get pulled inside the darkness. Since I was familiar with my pain body, I drew a line in the dirt and chose not to be dragged through it. I fought with everything within me to hold on to the edges of the deep hole I was in danger of being pulled into. I dug my fingertips in, and pulled myself, inch by inch, out of the hole. I didn't let it engulf me. This time, I handled the trigger differently. Knowing that the triggers I felt with Erick and Kevin were almost identical, I made a conscious decision to handle this breakup differently.

The next few days were tough. I went into hermit mode, which, as I shared earlier, is what I do after someone walks away from me. I avoid phone calls and texts and don't answer the door. Connecting to Source, I go to the deepest parts of myself and pray for the strength to get through a trigger. During these times, I've felt the coolness of my Angel's arms around my shoulders, loving me. When I feel that, I know I'm triggered.

I decreased my trigger in less time. Three days after our last text, I went to a Cosmic Convention, a gathering of like-minded people providing spiritual services. There are always more women than men at these events. I looked at crystals, jewelry, and Tarot cards and had two readings, which brightened my day. Yes, I was sad, but I didn't wallow in my misery, as I do. My energy was up and down, resulting in good and bad days, but my tears were decreasing. That was a win. I'm filled with gratitude for the valuable lesson I've gained. For me to walk toward healing, all this was necessary. Leaving the convention, I felt a positive shift in my energy. I knew I'd be able to ground on the greenway.

Chapter Twenty-Three
Revisiting the Past

On a sunny, warm May morning, Mother's Day, Ms. Zita and I made plans to walk on the greenway. Since the days are longer and temperatures are warmer in springtime, we walk earlier than on winter days, and it was a perfect day for walking. I was wearing my gunmetal camouflage cotton boot-cut pants with my thin, black, long-sleeved tee shirt and black sneakers. We completed our lap and said our farewells. Not long after she left, I saw a lady, Connie, who is a few years older than me, whom I enjoy talking to. I don't normally walk with her, but our conversation was good and my intuition prodded me to continue walking and talking with her. I didn't turn around at my normal spot, as we'd been sharing details of our lives. I saw four bicycles in a row coming toward us on their side of the trail, two women in front, two men behind them. Friendly and smiling, I said "Hi" to the two ladies. I looked at the man's face.

OMG, it's Erick! I can't believe I just said hi to Karen.

Erick had lost weight since I'd seen him the previous August, and he was wearing mirrored sunglasses, so I couldn't see his eyes. He was stoic. I said, "Hi." He didn't reply.

Did he see me before I saw him? If Karen had realized who I was, I think she would've gotten off her bike and confronted me, or worse. I was calm, and it didn't trigger me. I realized that except for having seen him at a red light eight days ago, I hadn't seen him for nine months—and that had occurred within twenty-five feet of the same greenway location, near the Grandfather tree. *He'd told me he'd been through hell.*

My head was spinning. I knew Divine had brought us together synchronistically. If I hadn't continued walking with Connie, I'd have been walking in the same direction he was riding his bike and wouldn't have seen him.

It was beyond coincidence and part of our Twin Flame Journey. Divine wants us to both do our part in our individual and joint journeys. Erick can deny this journey while trying to avoid our divine destiny for service to God and the collective, but I believe he knows he can't avoid our cosmic ties forever. Just as I do. What's divinely fated will happen whether or not we're together. I'll continue on my path and carry the load.

As I was contemplating this synchronicity, Sadie texted to invite me to come join in a family gathering.

☩

It was my second Mother's Day without seeing Roman. It had been a year since he'd moved to Michigan with Beth. I'd seen him during three visits during that time period. Last year on Mother's Day, he'd been gone less than a month. Now a dad to Lilli and Reese, he feels parental love from a different perspective. Even though Kurt still isn't speaking to me, I think of him and Roman on Mother's Day. I love them both, and nothing will change that.

Still in a funk after Kevin broke up with me, I wasn't sure if I'd want to be alone or to join Sadie and other family members on Mother's Day. After breakups, I don't want people to feel sorry for me. But I decided to go. *The situation is what it is. I'm trying to change my mindset and not live in the pain body anymore.*

I was positive that afternoon. Larry was also at the afternoon gathering, and he flirted with me like a schoolboy, shaking my chair and grabbing my ankle. I didn't react.

Seeing Larry reminded me I'd changed a lot since I'd seen him last. I was proud of myself for not falling back into an old flirtation pattern with him. I realized that everything I'd been through had contributed to my growth—I felt stronger and more sure of myself.

Recall that in a short period, several people from my past had reappeared. I'd seen Erick at a red light on Saturday. The following Monday, Chris, a man I was involved with after Erick, reached out to me, asking me to read his Tarot cards. (I did, and the positive cards showed he's receiving his "happily ever after" with his girlfriend.) Love was revealed throughout the reading. On Tuesday, Kevin had changed his social media status to single without telling me. I'd seen

Erick and Karen on the greenway, and then, on the same day, I'd seen Larry.

I wish I knew why they came back into my life within ten days.

I felt proud of myself for all the self-awareness work I'd done, especially the spiritual work I was continuing to do. Indulging my interest in spiritual and metaphysical subjects helped me get through the loneliest periods after my breakup with Kevin. So when a Catholic document was released on the topic of discerning supernatural phenomena, I wanted to know more. I reached out to Luke via text. Luke asked if I wanted to discuss it in person, and I said, "We can communicate through text." He said he would interpret the document for me but didn't follow through. My cards and pendulum show I'll never speak with him again.

Later, when I saw Sloan and discussed everything that had transpired, she wasn't sure what to say. On the evenings she stays with me, Sloan and I discuss things going on in our lives and spirituality. We've grown closer. In a few months, I'd watched her develop, and her energy is powerful. I told her I'd written a book and gave her a copy.

Sloan works two part-time jobs—one at an upscale retailer in town, and another is at our local library. One day at the library, she was reading my book when the library card cataloger saw her engulfed in my story. Sloan told the cataloger that I was sometimes her roommate and asked if they could add my book to their catalog. When she told me, I was apprehensive, given that the library is in the town Erick and I both live in. But believing that no one is brought into my life without purpose, I trusted God had brought Sloan into my life for a reason. I realized this situation had unfolded because Spirit had intended for others to read the book. I had a new copy of my book at home, so I prayed to remain protected by the Divine, and I sent it to the library for consideration. They added it to the catalog, and within a day, a library patron had checked the book out.

While I realized that my concern about revealing Erick's identity was real, I also knew that since I'm being called to rise as a Divine Feminine, and fear is a 3D illusion, I must turn away from fear. Would Karen see the book? *Possibly.* But it's been six years since we went to court, and neither Karen nor Erick would want to admit they're the people in the story. They both care about what people think. *Pride and ego.* Erick would fear his reputation as a pillar of the community being damaged and the exposure of our affair to his clients, community, family, and friends. Karen wouldn't want anyone knowing the circumstances of Erick's and my affair. I'd never intentionally out Erick publicly.

One day, Sloan walked in, her eyes huge. "You won't believe what happened." Working at the library that day, she was certain she'd seen Erick. When she saw him, Sloan felt a weakness come over her. We agreed she felt that way because she's read my book twice and felt close to the situation.

Then, two days later, Sloan came over and shared that she'd experienced something we both considered beyond coincidence. She'd been working at her retail job and was helping a customer. At the checkout counter in the small store, Sloan heard her boss call the name of another shopper: "Karen Smith."

Sloan told me, "It was Karen!"

"Oh my God," I said.

Sloan's boss had looked at Sloan and asked, "Are you okay? You look like you're going to pass out." Sloan said she'd felt ill and had to step outside. In my mind, that someone close to me who knows the story had encountered both Erick and Karen within two days goes beyond coincidence. Sloan and I sat in disbelief and tried to make sense of it.

Chapter Twenty-Four

Finding Soul Aspects

One day, while pondering my relationships with Erick and Kevin—and piecing together the similarities in the lessons I'd learned from each of the relationships, I realized the work we're all doing is soul work. I discussed this with Alana. "Because you've been working on self-love," she said, "it's allowed Kevin to come into your life." Then she brought up a topic I wasn't familiar with: soul aspects.

Aspects are people who share soul, spirit, soul families/soul groups, higher selves, and monads. I'd recently found monads are like a tiny, unique piece of soul that can't be broken apart. It's like a little spark of life that can think and feel in its own way. Imagine your monad as a box and your higher self is what's inside the box that holds the higher self. Some people believe that monads are connected to God or Source Energy. A difficult concept for me to comprehend was that our higher self has multiple aspects, which result in different parts of our souls that incarnate at different times on Earth.

I view soul aspects as comparable to a baseball team. Each player is an aspect of the team, yet each soul carries varying levels of the higher self. I draw an analogy between pitchers and catchers—the most important players on the team— and some soul aspects. Just as pitchers and catchers take on more responsibility in a baseball game, some parts of souls carry more of the higher self than others do. Each aspect of a soul comes here with similar lessons, has an individual soul contract, and their life on earth contributes to the growth of the greater soul.

Alana's insight and spiritual gifts amaze me, and she's always growing in her spiritual awareness. "I'm getting that Kevin's soul is an aspect of Erick's higher self."

"What?"

That caught me off guard. I didn't know this was possible, that two or more people can share the same higher self simultaneously. It was a lot to absorb, but I felt it to my core. However, it made perfect sense, and when I did readings with my pendulum and cards, the readings backed up her thoughts. *Wow! Kevin and Erick share the same higher self.*

"It makes sense because he's also a mirroring Twin Flame."

Erick and Kevin share similarities. As I mentioned earlier, both were raised in the Catholic faith. Both are loyal to family, are intelligent, and are successful business owners. They're both down to Earth, stubborn and manly, value fairness, love the same college and pro football teams, share a similar sense of humor, and have a similar vibrational energy I'm drawn to. They both have childhood wounds, have experienced trauma, and are damaged emotionally. Both have substance addictions and have been in trouble with the law.

I realized that my soul had drawn Kevin into my life as a replacement for Erick, both spiritually and in other ways. Besides Erick and one instance with Chris, Kevin's the only person I've seen through my third eye and have a strong connection with. It takes me back to the night when I asked God in earnest to help me move forward from Erick's energy. Over the last eight months, I've worked on letting Erick go. I still struggle with releasing the pain from Erick's actions, rejection, and abandonment. But because Kevin is an aspect of Erick, I accepted letting Erick go. I can move forward.

The idea of soul aspects resonated with my other relationships, too. For example, Alana said she believes Sloan and I are aspects of my higher self. (And Alana's channeling and pendulum reveal we are.) "You're calling your aspects in," Alana said. When I checked my pendulum and cards, they gave me the same information. Sloan's life has been difficult like mine, especially through childhood wounding. Every fiber of her being radiates love and compassion. When Sloan came to stay with me again, I shared this new piece of information. She was receptive and happy, as for her, it explained why she was drawn to me. I felt her love toward me—and I felt unconditional love for her. It made sense, too, that her intense reaction to seeing both Erick and Karen was because of her close connection with me.

Sloan doesn't have a social media account, so I shared informational social media reels with her from Coach Ryan, a Facebook content creator. One day, while I was scrolling, links to reels just showed up in my feed. His content focuses on attachment styles, specifically dismissive avoidant attachment. I remembered finding out I have anxious attachment, which allowed me to acknowledge my self-wounding better.

When I thought about things Kevin had said to me, I realized his contrary behaviors didn't all relate to Jane's narcissism. I'm not a therapist or counselor, but as I listened to a podcast, I understood Kevin has a dismissive attachment style. I watched more of the creator's reels. I saw Kevin differently—the reels explained his actions. According to Coach Ryan, dismissives value hyper-independence above emotional intimacy and have trust issues that correlate to childhood wounds. Dr. Sarah Hensley posts similar reels. Dismissives grew up with parents who didn't provide the depth of emotional support and warmth a child needs to be secure, and they can feel defective. Having had to learn to fend for themselves at an early age, they distance themselves in relationships emotionally. They deny the importance of closeness and intimacy. Suppressing emotional connections is a defense mechanism. Therefore, their relationships remain shallow. As a romantic partner, they can't be vulnerable because they don't feel worthy of love. When someone gets too close, trust issues come up, and, with a sense of relief, they pull away.

Triggering behaviors for a dismissive include a partner making big displays of emotion, being codependent, or pushing for communication. They dislike being controlled by a partner and abhor a partner making assumptions about how they're feeling. Their biggest fear? Abandonment. They feel unworthy, reject physical closeness (hugs, holding hands, sitting close, and sexual relations), and can be unfaithful. Also, while they refuse to offer genuine commitment, they can maintain relationships at a surface level. When overwhelmed, they withdraw and create distance from their partner. They fantasize about past relationships or they want to be single. When things feel serious, breakups happen.

This explained all Kevin's red flags that I hadn't interpreted correctly over the past year. Once I understood dismissive avoidance and anxious attachment, I discovered our two styles attract each other. I understood that all the things I'd done likely triggered him and caused him to run from and reject me.

I repelled him. Though I was unsure of his reaction, I wanted to share this with him in the future, when and if the timing was right. I believe it would offer insight. Letting the information sink in, I realized my friend Marie was dealing with a similar attachment with Jay.

One day, Marie reached out to me because a confusing situation had arisen with Jay. He'd pulled away from her, and she wanted me to read into the energy. Through the cards, we discussed attachment styles. The timing was no coincidence. Because I was aware of Jay's childhood and conflicting issues with his mother, I shared information with Marie about dismissive avoidant attachment. I told her Jay and Kevin both appear to have dismissive avoidant attachment styles. She'd fought for Jay, who was stubborn and shared similar behaviors to Kevin's. Our mirrored circumstances brought Marie and I back together. I told Marie I'd be attending an upcoming spiritual fair to get a reading into my situation.

Tasseography (Tea Leaf Reading)

Since my journey started, I attend local spiritual fairs when I can. One day, I attended a spiritual fair because several practitioners' booths offered helpful services. At the booth of an artist who channels portraits of spirit guides, I was first in line. As she drew, the first thing out of her mouth was, "Are you aware you're a healer?"

"Yes," I said.

She told me other things related to my journey and gave me insight into my past lives. When she was done, I had a charcoal drawing of a spiritual high priestess named Sewantas. Apparently, she has been with me through different lifetimes, especially in the East. Something about the drawing reminded me of my great-great grandmother.

Right after that, Bertena, a spiritual guide communicator who reads tea leaves, piqued my interest. Her art is called tasseography, and it fascinated me. She was wearing a flowing skirt, and her energy felt calm. Bertena invited me to sit in a chair.

"What question do you want to ask?" she asked.

She allowed me to choose a loose leaf tea to use in my reading. I chose rose bud. She poured water over the tea and instructed me to hold the cup in my hand. Then she asked me to drink it, leaving only a small amount in the cup.

I took a sip. It had an unfamiliar taste I wasn't fond of. I'm from the South, and I'm accustomed to sweet tea, not natural tea.

"Do I have to drink it?"

"Yes, you do."

I drank Ayahuasca. I can drink this.

Bertena suggested I sip the tea and ponder my question. I drank the tea but was careful to drink a small amount so I wouldn't swallow any of the buds. She told me that in the past, women did these readings by sharing their emotions and beliefs, supporting one another. I loved that. She asked if I'd swallowed any of the buds.

"No."

When someone drinks tea leaves, she said, it can mean their throat chakra is out of balance.

When Bertena saw the crystals I was wearing, she told me they were related to my heart chakra.

Yes, I'm wearing the ones to heal heartache.

Bertena turned my teacup upside down on its matching saucer and allowed the remaining tea to drain. Then she turned the cup over and looked at the top to see what I was eliminating. I saw an 'E' in the leaves. *This is going to be about Erick.*

"Something or someone with the letter E is leaving," she said. "You're letting go of something."

"It's my Twin Flame," I said.

"I'm sorry," she said. "The thing is, the leaves keep twisting and turning to the end. This isn't how they usually turn."

She showed me the leaves.

"See?"

It resembled a snake. The trail of tea leaves formed a circle, symbolizing a connection. She was unsure if it had ended or not.

"Whether or not you want it, you have the control. It's your choice."

She pointed to a shape in the leaves.

"But it seems like this person right here... is of the letter J backwards. The leaves keep morphing from a J to a L."

K is between those letters. Kevin.

Bertena felt I wanted to leave the situation. She said, "I want justice. I want love and fairness." Bertena said she's never seen the leaves move like that. She asked, "Did your Twin Flame break your heart?"

"Yes." A lump formed in my throat.

"Your heart isn't perfect. The pain is leaving your cup, and you're no longer going to feel it. Wait a day or two, and you'll release some of the pain." (It lessened.)

Then Bertena saw a white rose of protection in the leaves and showed it to me.

"It's Mother Mary and is protection and birth of new things." She mentioned it's time to create and heal. "There's strength," she said. "An angel with its wings behind it, so there's protection."

I leaned over and saw the angel with wings in the tea leaves.

Bertena asked if I had a question or intention.

I wanted to know about Kevin, but Erick was all over this reading. "Is my twin coming back into my life?"

"Here, it shows him circling back. I see protection and love, so you have the power to not allow him to come back. But you've the power to permit him to come back." Then she asked, "Is he coming back positively? Let's look at that. He's moving forward. He hasn't made his changes yet."

"I know he hasn't and isn't working on himself."

She asked me to look at a certain rose bud.

"The bloom is filled with love, ready to open," she said. "Love is down the road, as you're healing. The bridge isn't burned. However, the pain is still there. It's not gone from either of you. There was a trust issue."

Bertena had two beautiful Rebecca Campbell oracle decks. She allowed me to pick up the deck and shuffle the cards. The first card had the number thirty-four. It's a number I've seen for three years.

"What does it mean for you?"

I crossed my legs in my chair. "I don't know."

"Three plus four equals seven, and that's a spiritual, holy number. Yes. As a twin, was it romantic and business between you two?"

"Yes."

"And ego?"

I said, "He's still in ego."

Bertena saw it's still that way for him. "Your heartache is killing me." (She felt it.) She looked at me compassionately. "There's a lesson to be learned here."

You can't hide heartache from empaths. They sense it. "I'm tired of lessons."

"Right here's your beacon. You're going to be alone for a while and let your beacon shine. All this stuff's falling away. The only way they're going to fall away is for you to be alone. Shine and work on you."

"What will I do in the future?"

"There are many spiritual paths. Your face lit up when you talked about performing spiritual work."

I smiled.

"Make a list of three things you love."

"Although there's a lengthy list, if I must pick right now, Tarot, pendulum, and helping people. I'm also a healer and want to heal people."

She thought I'd succeed with my second book and spiritual business.

"You have a beautiful voice and heart. You're too kind for someone to treat you that way. You deserve to be loved 100 percent. That's part of this. When you connect with your higher self, your love, and the Divine Feminine within you, you're going to see so much of a difference, a different point of view."

After the reading, I asked if I'm supposed to read tea leaves.

"You can. Call me, and I'll show you how."

I thanked her and set up a session with Bertena, and she taught me how to read the leaves.

Chapter Twenty-Five

Looking into My Soul

Because I was struggling emotionally after the breakup with Kevin, Alana sent me for an in-person reading with her personal medium, Jessica. Imagine my surprise when I discovered I'd spoken with Jessica before, right after facing Erick and Karen in court five years ago.

It was mid-May. Jessica is a few years younger than me, with blonde hair and bright blue eyes. She sat in a chair across from me on her couch and held a couple of crystals in her hand while doing my reading. I mentioned the people who had made recent reappearances, and she told me Erick's role in our soul contract was to activate me, my higher self, and make me remember a different or higher timeline. She said we've had many past lives together. She channeled that there had been a betrayal in the past—in our personal lives and in business. Us coming back together in this life was an opportunity to clear that karma.

She told me that often, in a Twin Flame situation, one person activates and awakens the other. If the other twin doesn't do their work, the twin who does the work needs to accept that. Jessica said she feels I've accepted it and moved on.

Jessica asked if I still have feelings for Erick.

I looked into her white candle flickering. "Yes, although I've come a long way from where I was."

Jessica said, "You feel confused." She asked, "What happened with Kevin? Was the energy balanced? Did he look up to you?"

"His ex, Jane, is taking their son out of state in June. He's overwhelmed and pulled away."

She listened for her guides' help. Jessica heard, "He got triggered."

Tears filled my eyes. "Yes, I triggered him."

"You're a higher energy than he is," she said. She also channeled Kevin's words, "She's so much stronger than me."

I'd never thought about it that way.

Jessica said, "Something felt unbalanced. It's what's inside of him. His avoidant took hold, which was the way he exited."

"Kevin and you connected on a deeper level, and he got scared," Jessica said. "My guides say that there's a part of you that's torn about Kevin. You can honor and accept if you're in different places, but the heart wants what it wants." She told me she had an intuitive knowing we'd talk again.

I shifted my weight on the couch. "Yes," I said. "My Tarot card spread showed we'll talk again as well."

Jessica said, "Everything is coming to the surface. Things with you and Erick weren't resolved." She also heard and sensed Kevin's rejection. "His past came to the surface, and he didn't know how to open up." The breakup was an opportunity for him to do that. "There's turbulence," she said, "like a tsunami. It's the calm before a storm." However, she saw the water part and felt that was symbolic. "We're entering a new timeline where there will be clarity and peace." Jessica felt Kevin would contact me in three to four weeks and that things would settle in the next two to three months. She heard, "Kevin has desperation, grief, and sadness."

Confused about people from my past reappearing over the past month, I asked her why that had happened.

"Because it gave you a full-circle moment and an opportunity to be clear. When someone you love and care about (and they feel the same) exits your life, there's a chance to come back together." Her bright eyes looked into mine. "It's being clear with communication, trust, and respect. Everything needs to be out on the table. Erick's married, and there were things under the table, not able to be out in the open, and secrets, which were kept locked inside." Jessica listened to the information from her guides, then said, "It's been important for you to heal from that experience and be in partnership with someone you can open yourself up to and have a safe connection with. In your energy, it feels like a future and a path forward for Kevin and you. Is that correct?"

"Yes," I said. "He's been the only one I've been able to move forward with after Erick."

Then Jessica reverted to her earlier question. "Do you still have feelings for Erick? He still has feelings for you."

I replied, "We both do." Tears filled my eyes, and Jessica handed me a tissue.

Jessica receives metaphorical images that her guides give her. She had a faraway look on her face as she tried to explain what she saw. "It's like seeing a fly buzzing around your head, which is annoying for you," she said.

The energetic frequency Jessica received from her guides showed that I've made peace with Erick and what he chose.

I had to.

"He's with his wife and on that path," Jessica said. "You're on yours." Jessica said she didn't see Erick doing his work in this lifetime with me. She said, "You're moving on. Should he return, it'll be later. You'll be with someone else permanently at that point. You're acknowledging the love, sending light, and saying thank you. It feels peaceful for me that there's nothing. You're at peace with this situation and honor it for what it represents in your life."

Regarding Kevin, Jessica saw a timeline where we could end up together, and she heard, 'There's availability for reconciliation, but some things have to be addressed.' "You can't help him with that, and he might need some time to figure out what that is. Kevin may end up seeing someone else, but it's a quick fix. It's like an addict who doesn't want to feel."

She picked up on his past.

"He doesn't want to feel this, so he'll get back out there and maybe meet and date, but it's not addressing his issues. He looks up to you. You've done your work. We have soul contracts and we attract people who allow us to go deeper. We can heal within the partnership, or we get triggered and pull back because we're too afraid to face those parts of ourselves. He became avoidant, which is a form of disassociating because he doesn't want to feel what's coming up for him."

She picked up on his dismissive avoidance!

"It's fear," I whispered.

Jessica said, "He can't let himself be that vulnerable with you. At this moment, he can't. It's uncomfortable for both of you. He's hiding, and you're left with, 'Here I go again.' You're trying to make sense of how to move forward."

When I asked what the purpose of seeing Erick on Mother's Day was, Jessica said it was to remind me of how strong I am. I'm in a vulnerable place, and it would be easy for me to get sucked back into my heart being held captive.

Jessica channeled, "You've come so far to go back. You're not the same person." She said, "It's synced up to Kevin, because when he circles back, after feeling rejected, it can drop us inside a lower vibration where we self-abandon and make concessions that don't align with our truth."

I asked Jessica about Jane.

Jessica squeezed her crystals. She's the third medium that received lower vibrational messages about Jane.

Kevin's energy came through. "You're too good to be true," Jessica channeled.

She said that Jane doesn't like that Kevin was happy and felt she was threatened by me. It was something around "ultimatums," and his relationship with and spending time with his son. Jane was using me as leverage. Jessica channeled Jane. "Your son isn't a priority." Jessica said, "Jane felt restrictions around their schedule."

"Kevin's time that he could spend with me was based on how much time he needed to spend with David."

This made sense because Jane had kept their son occasionally when Kevin and I had dated, during the time he normally had David as part of the custody agreement.

Kevin standing up for himself is his lesson to learn, and it's painful. When I asked Jessica why Kevin had changed his status on Facebook to single, Jessica felt it was so that Jane would see it. Jessica said, "Jane is a narcissist, and they keep people under their thumb because that's where they want them." When people break free, narcissists don't like it. They do whatever they can to activate and punish them. She said he got activated after what I'd suggested sexually and became avoidant. Instead of standing up for himself or standing up for his feelings for me, Kevin retreated. Jessica said that we will discuss it when he comes back around and we talk.

"You matter," Jessica said. "It's not okay for you to be in a situation where the person whom you care for and love, and have given your heart to, won't make you a priority. That's non-negotiable. For your higher timeline, Kevin gifted both of you an opportunity to go deeper. Do everything within your power and don't go into the mind screw of being rejected again. This is the path he's chosen, and you're going to get clear you don't want to be with someone who doesn't make you a priority. If Kevin doesn't make you a priority, say, 'It won't work.' He'll be able to stand up to Jane one day, but it will take time, and he's going to fall on his face."

Jessica said she feels Jane was inappropriate with Kevin. "There's no boundary for exchange. Jessica thought he may be afraid of her, but he most likely wouldn't ever say that. It's unconscious, and Kevin doesn't have the energy to deal with it. That's the part of him where he becomes avoidant and retreats." She said Kevin's going to fall twice.

Jessica saw Kevin as distraught, in pain and grief, in a dissociative state, shutting down. "He can't deal with this and doesn't know how to make sense of it for himself. How's he going to make sense to you about it?" she asked. "This is unfamiliar territory for him. Kevin has to face trauma and pain, and you can't help him with that. This situation—it's like it had to come to a head for him to face his trauma. It doesn't mean you don't love each other, and it doesn't mean there's not a bond and connection, or that you can't come back together." Jessica said she kept hearing, "You're right where you're supposed to be."

When our session ended, I thanked Jessica for the messages and drove home.

Chapter Twenty-Six

Moving Forward

It was hard to sleep after Jessica's reading. After having endured several years of sleep deprivation, my dreams are less frequent. When I recall them, often I realize that they involve Erick, Karen, or Kevin. I hear Erick's voice sometimes—and it's beyond a dream. In small ways, my dreams have a prophetic quality to them. The first time Kevin and I separated, for example, I had a happy dream about him. We were coming back together. On the following day, he sent me a text. I've dreamed of Kevin, his oldest son, and Kevin's deceased father. In the dream, his dad talked to me, but I couldn't hear his words. A medium told me it wasn't a dream, that Kevin's dad had actually come to me in the dream.

One night, I was in the transitional, light stage of sleep. Through my third eye, I saw myself walking on the greenway. It was very real. I met Erick, and he looked directly into my eyes. It was like remote viewing with spiritual colors. I stopped and felt into the energy. It wasn't a dream. It felt like it did when we were together physically before I fully understood our Twin Flame connection—like my eyes were being sucked into his energy. *Had Erick experienced it, too?* I shared this with Alana later, and she agreed it had been a remote viewing experience.

One summer night, Alana asked if she could stay with me. When she arrived, I was happy to see her. With a big smile on her face, she said, "I have something to tell you."

My eyes were wide when she revealed she'd talked to Erick that day. She'd left him a message asking him to call her about a business matter. Until he called her back, Erick hadn't been aware that she'd divorced recently. The divorce had been amicable. Neither of them had had an affair—they simply fell out of love. She said, "No one should stay in a marriage if they're miserable. I think 90 percent of the people in this world aren't happy in their marriage and stay because that's what society expects. But I'm not that person. I want my happiness."

The best outcome for Alana is that she has remained friends with her ex-husband.

Erick asked Alana if she was interested in a CEO position within a medical practice. Alana told him she enjoyed her current company, because they're focused on God and service. That meant more to her than money.

Erick told Alana that making lots of money is important to him.

Wounded Masculines get caught up in earning money and equate their success to dollars earned. They push themselves, work hard, are successful, but don't see there's more to life than the bottom line.

Erick and Alana's conversation turned to how Alana and her religious sister are no longer allowing her to see her nieces and nephew because she's divorced. Her sister told Alana that she'd broken a covenant with God.

Why do religious people judge?

Alana shared with Erick that that's the problem with the church today, and he agreed. Alana explained to him she's more spiritual than religious. She said, "I see signs, and know that my guides and angels are all around me."

I learned that most of what Alana had said to Erick was to help him, and it was a nod to me. I'm grateful for our friendship and for her trying to help him see beyond 3D. As I packed to leave for the beach, I reflected on the conversation.

Here We Go Again

Sadie, her family, Larry, and I made it to the beach in mid-July. Knowing I'd see a repeating pattern emerge with Larry, I was friendly with him, but I had my shields up so the cycle wouldn't continue. It was the first time I'd done this with him, and as I expected, he started his schoolboy flirting again.

On the first night, during a waxing gibbous moon cycle, I was sitting on a chaise longue on the balcony under the near-full moon's light. Before the moon rose, I placed my crystals on the balcony for them to charge. Jamie, Ted's teenage son, came onto the balcony. Larry walked over, and we talked. Jamie looked at both of us and said, "Lovebirds." Larry shot me a quick look, but neither of us said anything.

I left the balcony.

After a full day of beach time, Larry got sunburned because he'd spent a few hours in the ocean and didn't wear sunscreen. His skin is pale like mine. As the ten of us looked at his lobster-red skin, I offered him some aloe vera lotion. No one else would rub it on his back, and Rae, Ted's wife, and others, insisted I do it. I've had deep sunburns, so I understood the pain he would have in the coming days. I applied the gel as gently as I could to his back and neck, and he jumped when I did. His exaggerated movements let us know he was overreacting, making us laugh.

Two evenings later, the night after the full Buck moon, four of us were on the balcony. Larry smiled and said, "I just want to be with someone."

That mini-triggered and upset me. I thought, *You had that with me eighteen months ago and chose not to stay.*

Later, I talked to my cousin Ted and shared my feelings. Ted said Larry had made that comment because he wants what Ted and Rae have in their relationship, but that he's a loner. The family all agree he will remain the same until Larry's mom, Bonnie, dies.

I stewed. I couldn't look at Larry. Not that I wanted to be with him again. In fact, after Larry's repeating pattern, he repelled me. To maintain a drama-free vacation zone, I said nothing. Telling him wouldn't have made a difference. Larry wants to have a beautiful woman half his age. He's a good person, but he has more hang-ups than most men.

The next night, four of us were sitting on the balcony again, passing the peace pipe, looking at the Buck Moon. The three men were talking about crazy women. Remembering that Larry may have referred to me going off on him four years ago, I said, "Women who do that have a good reason." Anger crept up inside me. "Women do that because of what men say or do."

Ted laughed in agreement. "That's right." He knows Larry and me well and knew I was being honest. Most likely, he remembered me going off on Larry by the bonfire.

There was limited surface-level conversation with Larry, to make the best of the time remaining on our vacation.

Later, Rae and I were alone on the balcony. She brought up Larry and said she supported us. *What? There's nothing to support.* I held my tongue so there was no drama. I don't think she knew I was mini-triggered.

She said, whatever "it" was, Larry and I have it.

Rae is implying that Larry and I have chemistry.

Words spewed out of me. "I'm furious at him. He disgusts me."

Rae said, "There's the two of you, and then you and him separate. He acts differently at a bar."

"Larry acts one way in front of people, as if he's a stud." When alone with me, he was gentle and respectful. "He's superficial, shallow, and wants a woman half his age," I said. "I was good to him when Bonnie was sick, and he chose his friends."

Rae said his behavior at the bar when he's with his pals isn't the same.

After two days, I could talk to Larry without my anger spilling over. Within a week, he no longer triggered me. The lesson I learned is that I've grown, and Larry hasn't. Larry may not want to be with me, and he isn't who I should be with. Anything that might be unresolved romantically between us with family was crystal clear at that moment. Any subconscious feelings that may have lingered were gone.

As I contemplated under the waning, gibbous phase of the Buck Moon, thoughts passed through my mind. *Larry would've been lucky if he'd stayed with me. But he isn't my perfect match. In the past, I accepted him, overlooking his patterns and behaviors. Larry and Kevin share similar attachment styles, but I think Larry is a fearful avoidant. I see my worth, and I won't doubt myself in the future.*

Free... at Last

This trip had differed from previous ones with family. It wasn't all lighthearted fun, with my internal drama, but at least the mini-trigger didn't engulf me.

Triggers happen, whether or not you're involved with someone. Time at the beach lets me release pain more and allows my soul more healing. As I sometimes do while sitting by the ocean in my colorful beach chair, I spoke aloud to Erick, hoping he would hear me telepathically. I told him I loved him (and me) enough to let him go. I released Erick fully. He'll always be a part of me. I was ready to walk away from the connection, and I wished him happiness with Karen.

People can have emotional attachments that can be negative. These attachments are like an energy cord. The deep fixation evokes feelings of being bewitched, mind, body, heart, and soul. If you want to sever the restrictive cords that bind you, visualize cutting them. I started this painful process during my past life regression seven months earlier, and now I snipped them unemotionally.

I said, "Erick who?" and smiled. *Free at last!*

Although the cords are cut, one golden cord will remain between us as twins. It can't be severed because of the Twin Flame connection.

Looking up at the night sky, and pulling my Divine Feminine quilt around me against the chill of the evening air, I acknowledged how far I'd come. With my choice to release Erick, peace came. God, my Angel Team, my Spirit Guides, and our higher selves are there for every step in my journey. They were there when I took roads less traveled and made choices that weren't in my highest good. They loved me when I didn't love myself or do the required work so I could graduate and not have to repeat a lesson.

It took thirty months after the affair with Erick ended for me to write about him in my first book. I was still triggered. I delayed writing about Kevin too, as I didn't want to walk into the familiarity of that pain. Along the way, I remembered good parts and wrote "Our Story," mostly with smiles. It included our first communication and ended with my healing at the beach. I wrote about the hard parts of him pulling away in two days—and I couldn't have done that unless more healing happened. A mini-trigger occurred when I was writing. Alana knew I was struggling and sent me healing Reiki energy. After that, I continued writing without incident. This was vital growth, and I recognized it.

When men have broken up with me, I've fallen into repeating cycles because I've tried to move forward before I'd healed from those relationships. I was lost, and my behavior was out of control. I no longer dwell on the thirty months after Erick, when I was on a self-destructive path. I can't change the past, but the experience helped me come full circle. I appreciate having returned to a gentle woman, closer to peace. There's no going back for me.

I drove home from the beach knowing I'd experienced tremendous growth and exponential healing during this trip... a work in progress. On the way, my intuition alerted me. Kevin would be in contact with me soon.

Our Story

When Kevin got in touch, it was because his mother, Wendy, wanted Mama's adjustable base bed that I'd offered her a few months ago. She reached out to Kevin, who texted me to set up a time to move the bed and other furniture. He also agreed to do a couple of things around my home for me. I told him I'd been writing. "Do you want to read what I've written so far?"

"Yes." After reading it, he said, "You have a detailed memory, which is dead-on accurate."

"Yes, I do."

After he read about our first date, he said, "Still the best first date I've ever been on."

As I shared more with Kevin, I told him I'd write about last fall, when things went awry between us, and that it would be hard, knowing writing about it would reopen wounds. Kevin reading what I'd experienced didn't change how I wrote. I shared that at the beach, I'd released Erick. I told Kevin, "I could do it because of your love, even after you pulled away."

Kevin apologized for his role in making my life difficult and said that hadn't been his intention.

I wasn't looking for an apology.

"Did you still want me to come over and help you?" He thought that by the time I'd finished writing everything, I might hate him.

I have some anger over the situation. "I could never hate you." We were communicating, and I asked Kevin if his therapist had ever given him a name of what his hyper-independence and trust issues were.

"No," he said. "Why?"

I summarized what had happened when the attachment-style reels came through my Facebook feed.

He was receptive to me sending those reels to him. He watched them and told me I was spot-on with this. He was baffled that no therapist had ever brought it to his attention.

After Kevin read the part in my book about us seeing the Bob Marley movie, he said, "That was a good night, and I think of it often."

Me too. The hard parts were coming. I dreaded writing about what had happened when he pulled away.

Kevin wasn't sure he wanted to be let in on the next parts of our story, but said he would leave it up to me.

Hoping to reassure him, I asked, "Why?" Yes, there was pain, but my healing also occurred.

One afternoon, knowing Kevin was coming to do a few things around the house and because he eats little throughout the day, to show my appreciation, I picked up dinner. I printed out the paragraphs of the manuscript I'd written and titled it, "Our Story." The latest pages included the words I couldn't take back, and I was aware this would be hard for him to read. But it's all part of the truth and was a big lesson for me. On the first page I handwrote, "Always know you're loved. Love, V.C."

He brought an employee with him to help move things. We didn't speak of our breakup while the employee was with him, but we both talked of hardships each of us had experienced while the worker was upstairs. When I went outside, I laid our story on the driver's seat of his truck.

Before he left, he hugged me longer than he ever had. He'd never given lengthy hugs, which I understood was because of his wounding and attachment style.

After I shared the tough parts of our story that had led to our separation, Kevin didn't give me any input. I'm unsure if he was struggling with facing his wounding, or if he had his own pain surrounding the events. Writing those words was a piece of my healing puzzle, and I hoped he feels loved.

Reflection

I think of Kevin in ways I've thought of Erick, and I send love and positive energy to him, hoping he receives it. My heart has mostly healed in three months, and he's the reason, despite his actions. Men often struggle with vulnerability, and I hope Kevin will open up in the future.

I've learned to let go of control. It was difficult before, but sometimes you have to move out of your own way, release and surrender a situation, and have faith that God knows what's in your highest good. This allows things to happen in divine timing. Divine orchestrated Kevin coming into my life, and it made all the difference. I continue to surrender and release our connection to God.

Before, Erick was my first thought when I awoke and the last thought I had as I drifted off to sleep each night. But that has changed. Yes, he still crosses my mind, but it's different. I pray he heals from his childhood wounds, adult traumas, ego, pride, and addictions. I now have firm energetic boundaries.

Releasing attachment to the outcome is by far the hardest lesson I've ever learned. After six years, I did it. I wasn't ready before to let go of Erick, but I also know divine timing has been involved in all parts of my life. I'm allowing my soul contract to play out.

Closing the Door

In time, Kevin reached out and wanted to come over in early December. We caught up. I asked, "Are you here to give me closure (between us)?"

He replied, "Not closure." He wanted to come the following weekend to do an activity together that required being vulnerable with each other. I was so happy he wanted that and told him I was open to it. He's in therapy again and working on his own healing.

We planned time together, but Roman and family arrived that night, so I asked for a raincheck. I realize now that as an empath, I took Kevin's wounding on as my own, without establishing boundaries. But I've washed my hands of it—it's his healing to do, not mine. Kevin isn't in a place for a relationship. He knows I'll be dating other people. He fell into previous patterns, so I walked away. Until Kevin heals, he'll remain in his toxic loop.

I'll never give my power away to another man again. For far too long, I allowed unacceptable behaviors from Kevin, and it all goes back to my time with Larry. I pulled away from Larry at the end of "round two" without being fair to him. I should've discussed in detail how he made me feel by choosing his friends over me before I pulled away, and changed the course of what could've been between us, instead of sending him the text I did.

Subconsciously, I overreacted to Larry's action and didn't want the same outcome with Kevin. Because of this, I believed everything Kevin said and didn't question him more. I let Kevin's behavior slide and didn't hold him accountable when I should've. Discerning this has made me reflect on my time with Kevin differently. It took me reading our story to see we both had repetitive, negative cycles. I still have an unconditional love for Kevin, but my boundaries are firmly in place. He knows this.

Upon reflecting, I realized I'd also been unfair to Larry eighteen months ago during Bonnie's recovery. Last summer at the beach, I was mad at him, so my thoughts and actions reflected my internal anger. This year at Easter, I saw Larry at our family function and told him I wanted to talk to him. We walked together from Ted's home to Sadie's house.

"You mini-triggered me at the beach last summer with your words. I felt you chose your friends over me when Bonnie was recovering," I said.

"I wish you'd told me about the beach. Two years ago, I was at a football event with friends that had been planned earlier."

I felt his regret. "I didn't think it would've made a difference."

Larry brought up me dating "the lawn guy." I told him what I thought he needed to know about Kevin, and that I hadn't been intimate with anyone since Larry and I were together. Larry said, "I would want you to go to church and not lay Tarot cards as much."

I didn't respond, as I'm not willing to give up the Tarot. But we ended the late evening with a warm embrace.

I'm glad we cleared the air between us. We're going on our family vacation to the beach in August. Larry knows I'm bringing along some aloe for him. He came over to do a small repair in my home, and I gave him a copy of the two chapters I'd written about him. I offered to update any parts that made him uncomfortable. Larry didn't ask me to change anything.

My last full trigger was well over a year ago. As a mirroring twin, Kevin had gifted me with my soul's necessary lessons to work on my healing. Even with all the hurt, our relationship allowed me to move forward and advance myself as a mostly healed Divine Feminine. I'm sure I'll experience mini-triggers from time to time, but I feel equipped to handle them better than before.

I've seen detailed "movie clips" through my third eye of Kevin and me being together in all ways, including intimately. I sense his energy with me in the same way I did with Erick. After Erick, I never thought someone could break down my walls. Other twins who struggle with this need to know it's possible. But it won't happen unless you work on your healing. Reclaim your own power. It doesn't happen overnight. Often, you take two steps forward and one step back.

I've asked God to bring in my true Masculine in perfect divine timing. Experiencing three divine connections within five years, I recognize my worth. I'll no longer accept breadcrumbs or a subpar relationship. The love I once poured into romantic partners is now love I give to myself.

How many mistakes can a person make? I've lost count, but over this past year, I've made better decisions. When things were difficult in the past seven years, I'd almost given up. God keeps intervening and showing me the way. Although this could've hardened me, it didn't.

Channeling

With Alana's channeling increasing, she's picked up on Kevin and Erick's energy, while giving me messages. With Erick, Alana picked up on chaos, pain, memories of what has been, and the inexplicable feelings he'd never felt before. There's passion, desire, and wanting rapture with me. She's also channeled Kevin's thought, "I didn't know it could be like this," meaning he's never experienced vulnerability and intimacy with the profound unconditional love that's within me.

Channeling is a connection and direct link to spirit. I plan to go deeper into channeling. This year, I'll start a spiritual business offering energetic healing and pendulum dowsing services, as well as Tarot and oracle readings. Most divinity tools interest me, but I'll continue to use my higher self's intuition and guidance so I'm in service to God.

Alana taught me how to create sigils—magical images created with the intention of producing a desired outcome. They serve as a divination tool. During the Lion's Gate portal energy, I used the four sigils I created. I used them to manifest selling my home, completion of this book, and personal goals. Intention and manifestation is something anyone can do. It may take time, but if it's combined with spiritual gifts, it can happen more quickly.

My spiritual gifts have grown, but I'm still working on having full faith and confidence in myself. I'm aware of five people I've helped through energetic healing. Healings include reiki (in person and distantly), physical healing, and clearing negative entities a few hundred miles away and from a home. Sending energy can be taxing. Think of it as exercising a muscle to become strong.

My greatest desire is to help and heal others, but my energy needs to remain high vibrationally. My goal is to not have energy dips, so I practice methods of raising my energy, including taking medicinal remedies that aid with spiritual growth. For example, while I've never taken psychedelic mushrooms, I'll journey with them in the future for personal healing. Psilocybin microdosing can help with addictions and mental health issues. It's helped Alana open her mind and receive high-level channeled messages from her spirit guides. I'm hoping for a similar experience. Our culture is changing to accept practices once considered taboo. So, be open to unexpected healing therapies, as it opens your mind to inner peace and your heart to self-love.

A New Attitude

We're here to love others unconditionally. As the airplane flight attendant says, we need to "Put our mask on first before helping someone else." I gave my mask to Erick repeatedly, without concern for my own survival. I now admit, I loved him more than I loved myself, and I was wrong. We need to give love to ourselves. Taking care of yourself first isn't selfishness, it's necessary.

I realized Divine put another soul aspect of Erick and Kevin in my life, as while we're just friends, he's protective of me. I'm how calling in my other soul aspects and Galactic family, and I wait patiently. Recently, I've met another one of my soul aspects. She's interested in spirituality, and I'm teaching her.

For the first time in my life, I'm focusing on me and my spirituality, without regard to any man. Although I don't want to remain alone, if a romantic possibility comes into my life, they're going to have to accept me and my spirituality. They must meet me in the middle. I know who I am… a force to be reckoned with. At the time of this writing, I'm thirty-two months celibate. A large part of me is my sensual power and desire, but for now, it remains contained as a reward for the right godly man. I miss intimacy, but I'll never again fall into trappings of having intimacy without a loving relationship. In the past, I short-changed and devalued myself and gave away parts that only someone who truly loves me should receive. As my aunt has reminded me, "You're the prize."

I've made bad choices along my journey. Most of them were after Erick walked away from me, when I was at my most vulnerable and on a self-destructive path. By the grace of God,

I survived to share my story. God forgave me. He could've forsaken me. Instead, God redeemed me.

I don't want to disappoint God. His love for sinners is something I don't feel worthy of. But I am. We all are. Sometimes I ask myself, "How was it I wasn't harmed in places I went, by people I was with, and in situations that happened?" The answer? Divine protected me.

This journey is a purification of the soul, and I've come full circle. There's no turning back. If I help one person make better choices by sharing my story, then I've accomplished my goal. If I'd internalized my feelings through what has transpired and walked alone without spiritual guidance, I'd have combusted. Those closest to me gave me love and support when I didn't feel worthy of receiving it. A few short years ago, I was a wounded Feminine. Now my goal is to be the best Divine Feminine I can be, and to challenge and empower other women to be a strong Feminine. I encourage you to maintain your boundaries and handle situations through extending unconditional love to everyone in your sphere.

These days, my spiritual mindset is peaceful. I have a thirst for remembering my past lives, fulfilling my soul contract, and accessing my deeper spiritual knowledge to share with others new to the spiritual path. I'm preparing for New Earth and my role during the transition, to assist others by teaching about spirituality and 5D unconditional love. During this time, people will be seeking knowledge, and others will remember what their purpose is. The spiritual veil will be lifted and removed permanently. There will be peace.

Wrapping It Up

A part of this book was given to me by my higher self, including the title. There are words within this book I don't remember writing. As I walked in the mornings, words and thoughts dropped into my mind and later, at home, those thoughts flowed as paragraphs when I typed my manuscript. This book was originally going to be titled *Reclaiming My Joy*. However, I healed sacred wounds while reclaiming my power. I challenge you to do it, too. Become a force to be reckoned with. Accept nothing less than you deserve.

I see Alana, Astrid, and me as spiritual sisters. We're in the same soul group, and therefore, we're family. I see us working with our other soul family members to facilitate and promote spirituality growth. Our biological family isn't always our "real" family. Our individual paths are intertwined, and we share a vision and will help others learn and heal others' wounds and traumas (although this isn't all we'll do). We'll teach others who are awakening (especially those awakening to the Divine Feminine) and starting their spiritual journey, as well as those wanting to know more about spirituality. Astrid and I have a spirituality podcast in the works to help others starting their own spiritual path, and Alana may be part of it. We'll introduce one topic and share things that have happened along our individual journey. Astrid will do pendulum work, and I'll pull an oracle card or Tarot spread for the collective at the end of each podcast. My story continues, and I hope it will help others. I'm open to possibilities of what my life will become. Having a psychic sneak peek through plant medicine, third eye visions, and intuition, my life is going to change in major ways. I'm stronger, mostly healed, and ready.

I send each of you love, gratitude, and positive energy. Go with the flow, and always know Divine supports you.

Unconditional love is the answer,

V.C. Pitt, Spiritual High Priestess

Epilogue

Mushrooms

As I mentioned, I wanted to try psilocybin mushrooms (magic mushrooms or "shrooms"), another type of psychedelic plant medicine. They come in different forms with varying shades of color. They can be silky white, yellowish-brown, bruise blue, and caramel colored.

On a Friday night five months ago, Alana stayed with me one weekend and brought some mushrooms for me to try. After fasting for a few hours, I tried a microdose with her. (There are microdoses (0.3 grams), social doses (0.5 grams), or a full dose (2.0 grams).) A so-called "hero's dosage" is between 4.0 and 5.0 grams. Sometimes people take greater quantities.

We called in our angels, spirit guides, and ancestors to guide, direct, and protect us through the journey. After placing our intent, Alana gave me a psilocybin film to place on the roof of my mouth. It melted. As with my Aya journeys, I had my Divine Feminine quilt, eye mask, and many crystals (including my pillar stones) with me. I lay down in my bedroom and listened to spiritual music, while Alana stayed upstairs in her bed.

After thirty minutes, I received visuals, which were gentler than they were with Aya. I saw many faces, including Jesus, some American Indian people, and women—my spirit guides. I've heard that some seekers see deceased family members during shrooms or Ayahuasca, but I didn't. The experience lasted two to three hours. Psilocybin is stimulating, so I didn't fall asleep until after 1:00 a.m. It was a tame experience, and I liked it.

Two days later, on a Sunday morning, Alana facilitated a psilocybin experience for Astrid and me in my home. She watched over us. We placed our intent. After we weighed the white psilocybin (with hints of light grey) mushrooms on a scale, Astrid took 1.0 grams and I took 2.0 grams. It takes a lot for me to chew and swallow a larger dose. It tasted like a rice patty. I swished a tiny amount of water around in my mouth to get rid of the nasty taste.

We wore eye masks and lay together on my king-sized bed. I had my spiritual clothing and jewelry on and my metaphysical accoutrements beside me as we listened to Ayahuascan music. Thirty minutes later, the journey began. In my third eye, I saw light code images similar to what I've seen with Aya, but with slower movements.

Alana came to check on us. I smiled and told her, "I wish you could see what I see." I felt connected to God's source energy. I was unsteady trying to stand (similar to my Aya's effects), so she helped me to the bathroom.

Astrid hadn't been feeling well in recent months. By its own force of will, my left hand came out from under the covers and waved healing energy toward her. I asked God to allow her healing. These words escaped my lips repeatedly: "Father God, the divinity within."

The Ark of the Covenant kept coming to me. Erick was in my heart, and I released a lot of pain through wailing. (I may have released him four months ago, but the pain from the situation remains.) With Ayahuasca, often, I sob, but this was different. I've let no one see me in that state before. Astrid and Alana are my sisters, and they love me, so I don't have to be brave or wear a mask around them.

Astrid said, "Get up. We've got to get out of here."

I told her, "I'm okay. It's the way I am. If you need to go, go ahead." I didn't realize at the time she wasn't in any better shape than I would've been to leave the house. She insisted, "You've got to get out of the sadness of this room." After some coaxing, I went outside to sit on my turquoise chair cushion inside my screened patio, in the sunny warmth of early fall. Still under the influence, I saw light codes against the brown vinyl on the ceiling. Astrid gave me a notepad and asked me to trace the codes I saw, but I couldn't do it. Not being able to draw them is intimidating. I hope to reproduce what I see in future journeys.

Alana is an all-knowing and wise oracle, and Astrid is a powerful warrior (she was a warrior before she incarnated here). Astrid knows I'm a high priestess, and Alana calls me "the Goddess." We're the power of three. We each have our spiritual gifts.

Alana asked me to come inside, and I did.

As part of her experience, Astrid told me later, she saw Aztec symbols on my face. I felt she was picking up on one of my past lives. When she'd said, "We've got to get out of here," it wasn't about her leaving my home. She saw our matrix breaking up. It was like the movie but with rainbow-colored pixels. Astrid saw different-sized squares, but the walls were disintegrating. She believes we've been living in this false paradigm far too long, and our 3D illusion was collapsing because we're overdue living in our reality. Astrid felt we've stayed here on the planet too long in this realm.

When we came down from the journey, we discussed what we had seen. When the sky got dark and the mushroom effects were gone, Astrid and Alana went home.

The next night, I lay on my side in bed. Glancing at my white faux window blinds, I saw black spots that appeared to be rain against the slats. The image transformed. It was as though I was watching an older movie with action. The blinds became Egyptian sand. The movement seemed to ride through the sand. I felt like I was remembering my past.

A month later, when I was on my own, I took a 1.0 gram dose. One mushroom was small and skinny and had a darker grey outline on it. That journey was a little scary, as I felt untethered from this world. I thought of Kevin, which kept me attached to my reality. When things get deep, I'm caught between two worlds. I took my eye mask off to reconnect with the physical world around me.

A few weeks later, I journeyed alone again and consumed a larger dosage. I reclined on my brown leather chair, covered by two blankets and with a heater in front of me. I put my mask on. I saw more feminine faces and enjoyed my journey. Through my third eye, I caught movement and looked up to see a DNA helix spinning above me. It was missing a piece. Like a magnet, the missing piece snapped into the empty space and the helix was complete. The Divine Feminine and Divine Masculine appeared before me, and their faces merged. I felt this meant that whatever piece had been missing inside of me was no longer incomplete. More healing had occurred.

I remember saying to God, "I step forward." The energy surrounding me was living and breathing. I glimpsed myself through Erick's eyes and felt self-love.

Two weeks later, Alana invited four members of our soul group to her home for a gathering. Alana's post-divorce home is warm and inviting. After dinner, we journeyed together. I took a social dose capsule, and I didn't go under fully—most likely because I'd eaten dinner. One member, Orlando (who sports amazing dreadlocks), has powerful positive energy gifts. Everyone was relaxed and enjoying our time together, but I was feeling anxious about some challenges I was facing. Alana gave me Reiki on her L-shaped cream couch. I sat quietly, tears falling.

Orlando talked to me and gave me a warm hug. Usually, I pull away from hugs before the other person does, but this time I didn't. My tears stopped. Since that night, I rarely cry. I felt he used his spiritual powers to take away the pain I was experiencing.

A month later, on a Sunday morning in late January, I prepared to take a 2.5 gram dose of shrooms. I texted Alex, a friend and classmate from school, to let him know I was journeying. Alana was at home facilitating journeying for other people, so I was journeying alone. I placed my intent and prayed for my safety. I asked that mine, Kevin, and Erick's higher selves be with me, along with the Archangels and spirit guides. *As we are connected in the spirit world, my journeys go beyond 3D and I need all the*

support I can get in 5D. I sat at my two-toned grey and black kitchen table, where I lay cards and do pendulum and energy work, and ingested my sacrament. My spiritual stones were close by, and I hoped for a gentle journey.

I lay down on my bed, opened an Ayahuascan playlist from YouTube, and waited for the plant medicine's effects to begin. Now in the 5D, I saw a kaleidoscope of colors, light codes, and many smiling Feminines, who were acknowledging my presence. I realized I'm part of something bigger—part of an intricate, web-like design. During the height of the experience, I saw Jesus (Yeshua) and Mary Magdalene about twenty feet in front of me. When He made his presence known to me, it was hard to stay in the moment because I wanted His loving arms to envelop me. I felt unity with Yeshua. There are no words to describe Christ Consciousness, but I experienced it. I became more spiritually evolved. My vision illuminated, and everything came together—and that hadn't happened before. I felt that mine and Erick and Kevin's higher selves were connected. The Divine Masculine and Divine Feminine were coming together, even if only in 5D.

I wondered if I was supposed to bring this back to the 3D, but when you come out of the 5D effects of plant medicine, you can't bring anything with you. Five hours after starting the journey, I went to the bathroom, leaned against my bed, and slid down to my carpeted bedroom floor and absorbed everything I saw. I lay down with my quilt wrapped around me and held my crystals. My fingers were swollen and tight, so I took off my rings—they were difficult to remove. My mouth and lips were dry, but my water bottle was out of reach. I was dehydrated and couldn't move. After six hours, I knew my physical body was in distress, which was alarming. I texted Alex, and he came by to check on me. I appreciated his concern. By then, I'd drunk some water and eat some yogurt. In the future, I won't ingest that amount alone.

After my journey, I channeled two songs containing the word *rapture*. A message I received clairaudiently that week was "Stay the course." I saw a large purple book made of dark leather with tattered pages. I believe it contained my Akashic Records. I hope to access it in the future.

Six months after my first journey, I took four social-dose capsules alone, which lasted a shorter time. Afterward, I had a conversation with Roman and Beth and recalled the same conversation from a clairvoyant vision that had happened a couple of months ago. I asked them, "Have we had this conversation before?" They said no, but I remembered it.

Alana and I journeyed together two weeks later. My dosage was 2.2 grams, which is what Alana's spirit guides said I should take. As I sat in front of the black sacrament bowl, I dreaded taking them. With each new journey, it becomes increasingly difficult to chew and swallow the mushrooms. The more you take, the worse the taste is, and the more you need to try to stifle the impulse to vomit. I almost couldn't keep them down.

Alana and I placed our intention for our angels, spirit guides, ancestors, and Jesus to come to us, while asking for safety and protection. Little did I know how powerful and sacred this journey would be. As I acclimated, Alana was beside me in her bed, because she planned on performing healing for me while in 5D. Alana asked to connect to my journey, and I allowed it and felt her hand on my left arm. Alana heard me say, "Father, Son, and the Holy Spirit," "Hallowed be thy name," "Thy kingdom come," "Thy will be done," "All that is Holy." "The divinity within," "We must save Mother Earth," and "They don't know what they do."

As I went deeper into my journey, I saw Earth as a fireball. It was flaming, and I realized our world was in impending danger. I pleaded with God, "Please save our planet. Please save our children." Luke's higher self came to assist me during this journey. Alana said my internal love was coming through to help heal our planet. Energy was coming out of my body. I called to Erick and Kevin's higher self, "I need you. I can't do this (healing) alone." My voice was lower. It sounded different and commanding. I felt mine and their higher self was with me. "Save the planet, NOW!"

After I exerted my full energy toward healing our world, I was overcome with emotion. I bawled, releasing more grief over Erick. It's what I needed. Full emotional release of grief is something I've avoided, but it's necessary. It's the last step of my painful healing process, although I know there's more anguish I have to let go of.

My body started coming down from the journey after four hours. This journey was different from the others. When you take the sacrament and it isn't capsules or film, the journey lasts much longer. Seeing our planet on fire was something I didn't expect. I asked Alana, "Did we come here to save the planet?"

She said, "You felt the pain of it." Alana saw caduceus wings across my body. I believe those wings are related to the physical healing I'll offer others. She felt my kundalini was activated, but it didn't rise up my spine. After six hours, someone drove me home. On the ride, I noticed distinct angelic images in the clouds. They moved and transformed. The faces of angels, Jesus, and Erick were in the clouds.

Hours after I came down, I was exhausted, and I closed my eyes while sitting in my recliner. I wasn't asleep. Jesus' smiling face was right in front of me. His face looked like the image from the Shroud of Turin, only in human form. His skin had an olive complexion. He hugged me. It was beautiful. I was overcome with joy and love. It felt like Jesus was proud of the work I did, and what I did during that journey had made a difference.

For three days, energy escaped from my body. My faith and love for humanity deepens with each subsequent journey. What you need to know is if you decide to take healing mushroom medicine, nausea can occur. For me, headaches linger for three days. The first two days are the worst. I have shoulder and back aches that linger for a few days. It's all worth it, though.

Two days after that, someone asked me to facilitate a first-time journey for her in my home. It was a unique experience. After performing a ceremony similar to what I've taken part in, I gave her one capsule. I placed my four protective moonstones at each corner of her recliner. Her experience lasted about two hours, and I watched over her. After her first experience, she said, "Your higher self was older and with me. You walked me into white safety." A word she heard was "mother" while seeing a triangle in her womb area. I felt she heard mother because it's one of the feminine archetypes, and she's a young mother. Jesus, whom she saw as very tall, also came to her and asked her to remember who she is. She felt Jesus was there because of me. Upon reflection, I believe I am to guide her. I'll facilitate for others in the future.

Psilocybin mushroom medicine is a tool anyone can use for healing. It's changed my life and has offered me more healing than I've received with Aya. The emotional chains that bound me are broken, and my mental anguish is over. My heart and mind are peaceful.

It's been over seven years since my spiritual awakening that began with my fall onto the tile floor. My journey has evolved. Love and compassion fill my heart. I'm focused on service to God and our transition to New Earth. I'm excited knowing positive changes are our end result, and that I'll play a small part in this future. I know that in the coming months and years, more souls will awaken, and spirituality will become prevalent. My sisters and I will assist others through their awakening and healing process.

Chaos is coming, and each of us will make hard choices. We must prepare. Light will win against darkness, and we'll shift to a higher state of consciousness and awareness with unity and unconditional love.

I'll leave you with this list of tasks.

- Accept
- Awaken
- Believe
- Connect
- Forgive
- Heal
- Live
- Love
- Meditate
- Pray
- Reflect
- Release
- Remember
- Trust

In Oneness,
V.C. Pitt

Appendix

Channeling

Through micro-dosing mushrooms, my friend Alana has connected with deities, including Mother Mary, Isis, and Kali. As I mentioned earlier, Alana's spiritual gifts are amazing. She gave me several high-level channeling messages over a month that explained my deep connection to love and why I've loved two men at the same time. Upon hearing the channeled messages, my internal focus shifted, and I'm focused on my mystical path. As I begin microdosing, I expect my spiritual gifts to increase as well.

Below are several messages Alana received and channeled for me from spirit guides that helped me understand myself and my soul contract.

We're here today. Love and light have been with you throughout your journey. We're here now to continue to guide and protect you. We've shown ourselves to you because of the completion of your book that we've assisted with. We're the representation of love itself between you and your twin. It's with great honor and love that we present ourselves. To fill your spirit as you write creates passion from within. This passion is shared among your readers and is your gift. This is our gift to you.

Continue to focus on self. This will propel you on your journey. Let go of the things that don't serve you. You can call upon us any time for guidance and clarity. Your twin will see us on your journey as you take mushroom medicine, which will occur soon.

My name is Armone. It means "the place that's within." The understanding that you see comes from within. You're love, and you're source energy. Hold on to this information when you question things. Trust that all has been taken care of. You're an angelic being of light, a warrior, the goddess of love. This is the reason. It's because you're the goddess of love that you can't understand why love isn't happening. Why is it so painful? It's because you love so big, and you've experienced such love in the past. It's why you asked for this experience in your soul contract. You'll have what you desire. Be patient. Patience propels you on your journey. The pain is suffering and inevitably brings you the love that you desire. We're grateful to provide this message to you today and to have the ability to communicate in such a way. It has been our honor to walk with you on this journey. We send you gratitude and love.

You're love, you're light, and it shines from within. You're spending your days filled with wonder of what's occurring within your life. All that's as it should be. Hold and trust,

hold on to that light, because it's your light that penetrates the darkness. It's where your anxiety and heartache stem from. Trust that all will be revealed. All understanding will be had. You're coming into your own. The process feels slow, but it's purposeful. Time must be allowed for things to occur as they may. You're the creator. You're of the Creator. You planned the beautiful web of this design in your soul contract. Reverse your focus. Focus on internal aspects of yourself and internal love. Fill your heart with the love of the goddess. It's within this love that real beauty lives. It's not until you find it you may move into external love. Although you seek to manifest external love on this journey, it isn't the focus. It's you loving yourself. We're the all. The all is divine. The all is all that is. It's one and the same. It's unity consciousness. It's oneness. It's sovereign, and it's unconditional love. You're the all!

We come to you on this day in wonder. We examine ourselves while we're on this planet. Examination is a virtue— examination within ourselves. Your spiritual growth causes possibilities for opportunities and continued learning and growing on the spiritual plane. Have remembrance of what we are, who our souls are, and what we want to be in this life. Most won't achieve this. In the days you struggle, remember this gift of knowing. You're the design and are of the Divine design, the essence. We come to you today with our hearts full, stream of consciousness, so that you may not feel alone. You feel alone, but you're never alone. We're always with you, always guiding you, always protecting you. Trust in this. The more you lean into trust, the more opportunities arise for learning. The more opportunities that arise allow you to be a servant to the collective, to be a teacher. The New Earth will be here soon, and it's your purpose to teach those who aren't on the spiritual

path. Your focus will be unconditional love. This is one of the greatest gifts of all on this journey. It's why you chose to be here. It's why you had this experience. Such pain is transcendence to this illumination of the light within. We thank you. We love you, and you're light. You're a warrior of light!

We come to you, to share with you our love and our gratitude for you being on this planet. The power of the all is within you, and the all that is. We're looking forward to you rejoining us in consciousness when you take the medicine soon. We're the bringers of light. We'll assist you on your next journey. We've been with you all along. You're the goddess. Continue to embrace her love, her power. Her authenticity continues to be strong in love and enjoyment. Your warrior will soon come to choose you and fulfill your desires.

Today is a day of great joy, calm, and peace. The completion of your book is here. It's our greatest hope that many will have the privilege of reading and growing from the experience you've set forth into this world. Divineness equals holiness. You're only beginning to find your divinity. You've only yet tasted it. The more you believe in yourself, the more the feeling of the power of the goddess grows. This love you're pushing out into the world changes it forever. It affects other timelines and dimensions. The way you push out your energy, do the same for drawing in your aspects to you. Instead of pushing energy, pull it in and visualize it coming back within your body. This pull and visualization may take time, but it's needed to invoke your entire power and to change the negative energy that exists within your lineage.

The higher calling is from the higher realms, where your higher self exists in completeness and wholeness. It's where your twin and mirroring twin are as well. All three of you, the triad (the Trinity) forms a pyramid, and the tribe is coming together. You feel it. It goes back to the power of three. Although your tribe is much bigger, right now it's focused on only three. Allow yourself grace, gratitude, and encouragement as you continue forward on your path. Some of your tribe may seem to progress on their journey faster than others, but that's not the case. We're the way showers, the guardians, the bringers of the light that will help others find their light. It's our heart, our passion, our love, and our joy to connect to the all in such a way. It's with bravery and honor that you came here to this planet. That you chose this experience. Call in your Galactic family daily. Ask for their guidance; ask that they show themselves to you. This is your next step on your path. Besides the mushroom medicine that you'll soon take, you wear a beautiful crown upon your head on your home planet. It's why you feel connected to the word "goddess."

Alana spoke while she channeled the next message for me, so below is a combination of what she saw and the message itself.

Oh wow. I can see you. You look so beautiful. You're radiant. Your skin is glowing like in the movie Twilight. You're wearing a white iridescent gown that flows behind you. It's long sleeved, a V-neck. Your hair is longer. You're younger and so beautiful! Your higher self is drop-dead gorgeous, and your heart... wow. I can sense it. You're sending it to me now. Gosh, you love so big. I see you, the love you have for one another. Your higher self is letting me sense it. It's incredible. This is amazing. I see that you've got your arms crossed like you're hugging yourself, and now I'm able to connect to your energy. It's the way the medicine has been teaching me. I can see you inside my head. Your face... you're smiling at me, and your hair is red. I feel your thoughts racing. You're trying to distract yourself, but all those thoughts are still there. When I channel, I take on the individual's expressions, sometimes their laughter. I smiled like you. I'm seeing a web, an energetic connection. I can see the web from you to Kevin and Erick. It's the energetic triangle that we talked about before and comes out of your heart chakra into theirs. It passes through all three of you, which I find interesting. There's a longing there amongst the three of you to find your soul and to connect. You've helped each other do this so many times before. Oh gosh, all of you are sending me the love you feel for another. It's precious. My heart is swelling up inside. You have pride for what the three of you have accomplished in these other lifetimes. You're all smiling, because you understand the higher perspective and how things must work and flow. Oh gosh, this feeling is so wonderful. You're telling me how much you love me. I took on your smile again. You're looking at each man, smiling with connection and joy. Your higher self is saying, "Keep the faith."

Your hair is blowing in the wind. It's back to your goddess vision now with the white dress, with all the beauty and the love. Your higher self wants you not to limit yourself. She wants you to not make statements like, "Here's what I want, but I can't because of this." She's telling me you're limiting yourself by stating things in such a fashion. Change your perspective. Change how you speak. Change your thought process. I hear the guys say, "We love you, my love." We're always with you, always protecting you and always loving you, even if not in the physical. You're our everything!

⚓

We come to you today with peace, love, and well-being. We're of the Pleiadian collective. It's within this time that we acknowledge and give gratitude for the work you've done while you've been on this planet. You're a high priestess. You've made quite the journey to be on this planet. You bring within yourself a frequency to raise the vibration of the planet and the inhabitants on it. It's a great responsibility that was given to you. We regret to inform you, it's time for us to leave soon. You'll be here longer. There comes a time when we must prepare this planet to raise its vibration and expand its consciousness. This will be a time of chaos on this planet. You'll stabilize, but it will be difficult. Although this is your mission, it isn't one of high regard to experience in the physical. It's the warriors, like you, that decided to come to Earth. This you've known and felt. It's why you know you're not from here. This isn't your home. This isn't where you belong, but you heard the call. You're tired and weary. Your nervous system is affected by the negative influences on this planet. All will be well in due time. Your internal infrastructure will be rebuilt. Your internal program will be rebooted, so to speak, with the fresh energies and expansion of consciousness and vibration within this planet that must occur for the planet itself to raise its vibration and consciousness. It's with great love and great tidings that we honor you today, that we send you gratitude for your bravery for you coming to this planet. We await your return.

There's a time and a place for love in the way it should be in 3D. It's not like 5D, where unconditional is all that is. It's a complication for you when you remember 5D unconditional love and want that in this reality. For you, this is the case.

It's why you struggle. This time shall pass. However, in the 5D, love will become a reality soon for all on this planet that are still here after the New Earth transition. It's important for you to remember how special you are. Only the greatest and bravest of warriors are here at this time, to raise the vibration, to be of service, and to push out the energy as unconditional love. Lightworkers on this planet are bombarded with negative energy, drained from others who have negative energy. Acknowledging this helps you understand it and transmute it. Being in nature is one of the best ways of transmuting energy. It's why you like to walk and become stressed when you can't. When it isn't the season for walking, find other ways to achieve the same goal. Embrace yourself in all ways with joy, love, grace, and gratitude for all you've achieved. You're exactly where you need to be on your spiritual path. We're here supporting you always.

At the partial lunar eclipse, let us focus now on Aphrodite and your connection to her. What does this mean? How does this affect you? It affects your knowing in a way that's somewhat indescribable in human form. It's strength, love, forgiveness, and meaning all wrapped in one. You've worked with different archetypes or goddesses throughout your entire life here, sometimes knowing and other times unknowing. One must be on the path to enlightenment to have knowing. Aphrodite can be your inner strength, and she can be your guide. You're one and the same with her when you tap into her energy. You can channel her as well, if you so choose it and ask for it. You'll feel her words coming through differently as you speak or as you write. It's in those moments that you sense the highest of connection. You've been doing it without realizing it. Aphrodite has a very sensual side of her as well. Feel this

and know this about yourself, especially in times where you aren't connected in the physical world with another. Aphrodite is a reincarnation of many beings, and many beings are a reincarnation of her. You can research and determine what incarnations exist, then tap energetically into those goddesses as well by saying their name. Ask how they relate to your Akashic records. Ask daily to see the records. Create a sigil for reading your Akashic records. This will assist you in connecting in the way that you would like.

BEFORE (206 LBS) / AFTER (145 LBS)

CRYSTALS USED DURING A HEALING SESSION

CROSSING THE FINISH LINE AT THE RUN

ON TOP OF RACHEL'S KNOLL

INSIDE THE CHAPEL OF THE
HOLY CROSS

HOLDING REESE AND LILLI
FOR THE FIRST TIME

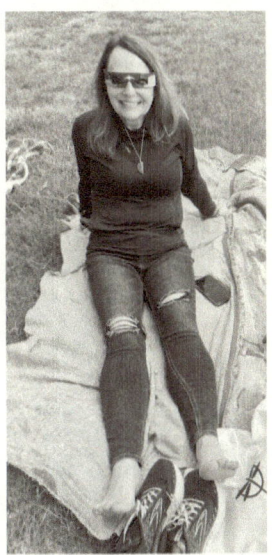

AT ANGEL MOUNDS BEFORE
THE SOLAR ECLIPSE

ALANA, ME, AND ASTRID

SLOAN AND ME

Bibliography

Books:
Tolle, Eckhart. *The Power of Now: A Guide to Spiritual Enlightenment.* Vancouver: Namaste Publishing, 1999. Print.
   ---. *The Power of Now: A Guide to Spiritual Enlightenment.* Novato, CA: New World Library, 2000. Audio.

URLs:
www.elohee.org

About the Author

V.C. Pitt recently moved back to the county where she grew up. She became a grandmother and loves spending joyous time with her twin grandchildren. This is V.C.'s second spiritual memoir, the first being *My Twin Flame Journey of Separation, Surrender, and Release*. She's now three years post-breast cancer and participates yearly in mud cancer runs. V.C. lives her best life by walking and being in nature. In recent years, she's evolved into a Spiritual High Priestess and loves sharing her spiritual gifts and wisdom. Always evolving, soon V.C. will start her metaphysical business and offer Tarot and oracle readings, pendulum dowsing, and energetic healing. Her intention with this book is to introduce others to spiritual modalities and plant medicine and to help Twin Flames and others let go of triggering emotional pain to release deep-seated mental grief.

www.ingramcontent.com/pod-product-compliance
Lightning Source LLC
Chambersburg PA
CBHW021711120626
46545CB00004B/1513